A Design for Social Education in the Open Curriculum

A Design for Social Education in the Open Curriculum

Shirley H. Engle
Indiana University

Wilma S. Longstreet
University of Illinois

Harper & Row, Publishers
New York   Evanston   San Francisco   London

Contents

Preface

The traditional approaches to social education are no longer sufficient. The explosion of knowledge, the swiftness of change, and the range and complexity of modern social problems require a continual updating and reinterpretation of the social data available to the citizen. Social reality does not fit neatly into pre-established topics nor into the disciplines nor into the pedagogical subjects which flow out of them. The ability to interpret changing situations and complex social data must be the paramount attribute of the good citizen in a modern democracy. Consequently, the development of this ability must be the core of social education.

A curriculum based on the transmission of a few of the social science disciplines, as is generally the case today, not only gives a skewed and incomplete notion of reality, but so fragments the study of society as to render it irrelevant to daily living. Social education, as it is practiced today, is rightly accused of being extraneous to life.

This book proposes an approach to social education which, by focusing on the full range of data sources, media, and forms of human action, promises to make the curriculum relevant both to the individual and to society. Action-concepts defining the full gamut of situations in which human beings act in either a personal or societal sense afford the structure for curriculum development. Students are involved in coping with heterogeneous data much as they would in life outside the school.

This book does not purport to outline the detailed content of a total curriculum. This can only be done by the students themselves and by their teachers in the daily arena of life experience. It does afford an approach to curriculum which promises to yield a well-balanced, logically powerful, and relevant curriculum.

Envisioned as a sequel to this work is the development of supportive materials covering the gamut of resources, including the social sciences, history, and the direct experiences of youngsters. Within the framework provided here and with an abundance of materials available, the teacher and students will be able to make choices effectively leading to the development of their own curriculum.

Shirley H. Engle
Wilma S. Longstreet

A Design for Social Education in the Open Curriculum

1 Where To with Social Education?

THE DISCIPLINES AND THE PROBLEM OF RELEVANCE

We in education are hung up on the disciplines. The reasoning follows along these lines: Organized knowledge has yielded man the greatest control over his environment and the greatest promise for increased control in the future; the disciplines are the maximum culminations of organized knowledge and have proven their worth across the years; it is, therefore, reasonable to make them the basis of that learning which a highly complex society intentionally passes on to its young. The subject, which is the pedagogical reduction of a discipline so that it may be learned more easily, has been the primary educational form used in the school.

We have allowed ourselves to be impeded in several ways. In recognizing the value of disciplines, we have unconsciously accepted the disciplines as the only source of organized knowledge. In so doing, we have ignored the fact that most of the decisions we make in our daily lives are neither referred to nor guided by the disciplines. Moreover, and importantly, the average life is not lived in chaos. Human beings organize and reorganize their experiences in logical configurations suitable to their life needs. Such configurations do not necessarily fit into a discipline. For instance, common sense and intimate feelings interact with social experience to yield models or beliefs for acting that may achieve desirable results for the individual but that cannot be placed in one or even all the disciplines. From the moment of birth, the individual is engaged in organizing and classifying his experiences in the effort to make sense of the world about him. He sees the world as a series of questions, topics, and problems, not as disciplines, which are categories contrived by scholars to achieve knowledge free of time and place. Those sources of influence that guide everyday living but that lie outside the disciplines tend to be ignored by the schools. Much of the cry about the failure of the schools to be relevant arises from this neglect.

The second obstacle is our failure to recognize the intended functions of the disciplines. Disciplines are developed as ways of analyzing, in greater depth, the component parts of existence. Each discipline concerns itself with a small and intentionally isolated segment of existence. As more knowledge is acquired, disciplines tend to subdivide themselves in order to achieve even greater precision of understanding. Thus, while increasing in number, they decrease in scope. The claims made by the scholars of any one discipline are always qualified by the statement, "Everything else remaining the same," a condition nonexistent in human society. Knowledge derived from a discipline is highly fragmented, abstract, and theoretical. Each discipline, studied alone, without attention to other disciplines, gives an incomplete and, consequently, distorted view of existence. This distortion is further compounded in our schools where study is limited to fragmented parts of a small number of disciplines.

Furthermore, the gains we have made in the psychology of learning in recent years have been applied immediately to the better teaching of subjects. Thus, the work of Bruner, Skinner, Gagné, and others has been applied almost exclusively to the learning of disciplines, while human situational learning has gone uncultivated. The inquiry method, programmed learning, team teaching, and the like have been used primarily in what is proving to be a largely fruitless effort to increase the efficiency of teaching school subjects.

If we accept that organized knowledge may be derived from other than the disciplines, we must then decide whether the disciplines offer the most desirable basis for school study. The objective of the subject structure is to simplify the content of a discipline for instructional purposes while maintaining a close replica of its actual form. The subject is justified within the educational context only if replicating the discipline is considered of primary importance to the learning goals of the school. This primacy was challenged (though never overcome) at the very beginning of the twentieth century, when the psychological needs of the child and the effective relating of the child to his community were set forth as far more significant goals of education. Human situational learning was given preference to the stress on disciplines. The organization of information around a topic, especially the social problem, was offered as substitute for the discipline-oriented subject.

Discipline-based subjects, even when related to the most exciting developments of the times, remain impersonal, value-free, and fragmented studies that require abstract operations based on previously established principles. The student may be led in school to discover these principles himself or he may be given them. In any case, the confrontation with the heterogeneous factors invariably involved in the daily situations of his life is avoided.

The willingness and the ability to deal with the concerns of the individual may be achieved through the topic, which can draw its content from a varying number of disciplines as well as from no discipline at all. The topical approach is capable of relevancy from the standpoint of the individual. The discipline-based subjects achieve relevancy from the standpoint of the society as a whole. For example, the demand for space scientists reflects a societal need, and the school, consequently, stresses physics, which may eventually produce for society the space scientists it requires. However, the individual, although influenced by societal needs and scholastic emphasis, will achieve his dedication to disciplines upon the basis of personal decisions rooted in the everyday affairs of his life. Clearly, there exists a relationship between situational learning and the study of disciplines. As an instance, if the individual has become concerned with pollution and has topically dealt with it in school so that the importance of biological knowledge has been stressed, he may well want to gain command of biology as a discipline or even as an occupation. In this fashion biology is not just societally relevant but personally relevant as well. This suggests the introduction of disciplines at any point in the curriculum of the individual when personal relevancy has been achieved.

We are dealing with two diverse forms of relevancy. We have, on the one hand, what is relevant to the individual, represented by his questions and concerns, and, on the other, what is relevant to society, represented by the teaching of disciplines in the school. The educational alternative lies between organizing the curriculum in response to the questions and problems which arise naturally from the life of the student, and organizing the curriculum around a *few* of the disciplines thought to be of most social significance.

Because both aspects of relevancy are proper goals for education, it may be argued that there is no need to make a choice. To say that the schools can cope adequately with the needs of both personal and societal relevancy is frankly impractical. The already proverbial explosion of knowledge shows no signs of lessening. The subject-oriented curriculum design may multiply the number of subjects available to students, but the number of subjects that a student is able to absorb has shown no signs of increasing significantly. The retention of the subject curriculum has meant the increased "piecemealing" of learning. This "piecemealing" has gone on not only among the subjects but within the subjects as well. We have already given up hopes that even one discipline might be "completely" learned by an individual. The societal relevancy that can be attributed to the subject design is no longer tenable in the wake of a multitude of newly elaborated disciplines. The disciplines may be a necessary part of the advanced education of the student intending to specialize, but for the student who has not yet made up his mind, the accent on the disciplines can only mean that there will be less time for the schools to help him think about the meaning of his own life and of that of his society. This is not to say that the study of disciplines should be eliminated, but rather that they should be delayed until such time as the individual student sees their relevance. It seems more useful first to excite a sense of personal relevancy with regard to physics or economics or some such study and then encourage the in-depth acquisition of the discipline, rather than to force youngsters prematurely to study what appears to them to be totally unrelated to their experiences and concerns.

Despite the general recognition of the importance of situational learning and personal relevancy, we continue to use the subject design almost without exception. Not even in the social studies, an area originally developed to escape the limits of the disciplines, have we faced our choices squarely. The social studies, labeled a subject in our schools, has come to be treated more and more as if it were a group of disciplines. Thus, even the social studies have been made so impersonal as to be unreal to the student. The personal needs and problems of the young are still treated as incidental concerns, while stress is placed on an abstract kind of knowing associated with the disciplines. Immediate personal relevancy, which must be based on the interests and involvements of the young in their everyday lives, continues to be systematically ignored in favor of discipline-oriented subjects.

It is necessary to organize information around topics if we are to accomplish a curriculum that makes sense to the individual. Topics may be interdisciplinary, drawing their content from various domains including the social sciences. The mere decision to organize a curriculum around topics does not, however, ensure personal relevancy. Topics, like subjects, can be imposed upon the learner from the top without considering his interests, problems, and concerns. The topical approach merely makes it possible to achieve personal relevancy in the curriculum.

The topical approach has not been without its own problems. The increased personal relevancy promised in the topical approach has not been sufficient compensation for the loss in organizational power offered by the subject curriculum. The selection of topics such as "Poverty," or "Pollution," or "What Do We Hope to Gain from Life," does not automatically suggest the structure or the intellectual tools needed for rigorous study, nor does it provide for sequential development of learning experiences. For instance, under the general topic of pollution, the biological imbalances created by man could be studied, or how one's own city is being polluted and what can be done about it, or industrial efficiency versus a livable environment. Indeed, the range of content that could be involved and the techniques of investigation that could be used in studying topics are so open to variations that any hope of the public schools achieving a logical ordering of learning experiences from one level to another and from one teacher to another would have to be abandoned. What is needed is an intellectual structuring of topics that would ensure their systematic study. Structure is required which will provide for the sequential development of knowledge. It is the claim of this work that such a structure is provided by what we shall refer to as the "action-concepts."

THE SOCIAL STUDIES DISTINCT FROM THE SOCIAL SCIENCE DISCIPLINES

The social studies could have become that part of the total curriculum that was designed to cope with personal relevancy. It was intended to be the social education of citizens. Instead it has remained a nebulous concoction of disciplines dealing with human behavior in an objective and value-free vacuum. We have avoided making choices regarding our goals and our structure. Are the social studies merely the reduction of social science disciplines for pedagogical purposes or are they to include the comprehensive social education of citizens? Put in other terms, the question is whether the disciplines are a sufficient source of input for the social studies or whether new sources of input must be sought. Are the disciplines alone adequate for the individual needs of citizens? This is an old issue, dating back at least to 1916 when the Committee on the Social Studies of the Commission on the Reorganization of Secondary Education of NEA declared the development of social efficiency and good citizenship to be the goal of the social studies. Ambiguity and confusion on this point have persisted to the present.

The very real curricular differences which result between an interpretation of the social studies as the teaching of social sciences and an interpretation of the social studies as social education have not been squarely confronted. Most of the projects which have come to receive the deceptive label of the "new social studies" are concerned primarily with updating and improving the teaching of social sciences. Almost none of these funded projects have been concerned with improving the comprehensive education of citizens. They, like most of education, have bogged down in the disciplines.

To a large extent, we may have been deluding ourselves into believing that we have grappled with an adequate structure for citizen education. Integrated courses in the social sciences have frequently been labeled social studies. Such courses do not meet the requirements of a discipline, for they are too profuse and unstructured to do so. Nor do they meet the needs of citizenship education, for the myriad of problem-solving situations which the average citizen encounters are but poorly coped with in a structure based on the disciplines. Integrated social sciences, furthermore, carry with them the same characteristic of their more specialized components, which is the avoidance of value problems. The social scientists, in their effort to achieve knowledge outside of a particular context, disclaim any special interest in the development of values or, for that matter, citizens. Yet, it is impossible to treat topics which are relevant to us personally and to our times while omitting values. Integrated or fused courses are hybrids that have for too long deceived those who believe citizen education and the utilization of knowledge in meeting life situations should be the primary goals of the social studies.

The conception of social studies which would make them no more than the social sciences simplified for scholastic learning is highly deceptive. The problem lies not only in the narrow treatment of the social studies but in the failure to distinguish between social science teaching and social science research. The social scientist is essentially a discoverer and organizer of new knowledge. In this role, he is a skeptic of all knowledge, holding his own conclusions tentatively. This is lightly passed over in most social science teaching, which is mainly an effort to teach the findings and conclusions achieved through research. One of the glaring defects of such teaching is the almost certain obsolescence of its content, for the teaching field inevitably falls behind in the explosion of knowledge to which the social scientist is continually contributing. It is time that we properly distinguish between the research function of the social sciences and the teaching of the social sciences. The expertise of the social scientists is not pedagogical; they do not make this claim.

Another shortcoming of the notion that the social studies are the social sciences simplified for pedagogical purposes is the inadequacy of the social sciences, when taken alone, to fulfill the need of citizenship education. This is not to say that the social sciences are not an important part of the education of citizens. It is merely to say that they are not a sufficient basis for such education. To make the social sciences the sole basis of citizenship education is to place values and the valuing process outside the pale of social education, because the social sciences are value free. To make the social sciences the sole basis of social education is to accept those models which have proven successful in scientific research as guiding models in the complexities of daily life. It is a way of treating our daily problems piecemeal, for no social science, taken alone, describes more than a fraction of human behavior. Each social scientist assumes as he works that all else remains the same, an assumption generally ignored in the teaching of the social sciences in the schools. We know that all else does not remain the same. To pretend so is to rob the student of necessary experience in synthesizing and resolving the conflicts between the various models provided by the social sciences, as these would operate in real social situations.

The social sciences are not intended to be personally relevant. Theirs is a societal endeavor based on generalized patterns of human acting as these occur, without any reference to the desirability of their occurrence. The effort is to achieve objectivity beyond that which any individual could attain. There is no doubt that this is societally valuable. However, even when the citizen takes into account the objective conclusions of the social sciences, he still must make personal decisions. These decisions always involve his values, his heterogeneous experiences, and the amalgamation of the pieces into which the social sciences divide the study of human behavior.

THE TOPICAL NATURE OF THE SOCIAL STUDIES

Citizenship education must necessarily be topical. It must place its focus on the utilization of knowledge from all sources so as to adequately meet the multifacet situations that confront a citizen. Citizenship is not reflected in the disciplines with their concentration on a minute area of understanding. The citizen must operate on a complex interweaving of frequently unpredictable circumstances. The topical approach reflects both the unpredictability and the personal relevancy involved in citizenship while still permitting the instrumental use of the disciplines. The topic can most closely parallel the life situation of a citizen outside of the school.

But even if our choice has been made—that is, we accept citizenship education as the proper goal of social studies and we accept the topical design as that pedagogical approach which can best reflect the interactive, problematic-type content upon which relevant citizenship education must be based—we are still faced with several fundamental decisions. What should be the objectives of a social studies course with regard to the student, the particular social situation, and the society? In other words, how is good citizenship conceived? What are the proper roles of citizens? In the light of these objectives, what would be the sources for the selection of topics? Can a curriculum design be achieved which would be a powerful instrument of pedagogical organization and yet retain the flexibility of the topic? How can balance be achieved between situational flexibility and preconceived pedagogical structure?

These questions, to some extent, pervade the entire field of education. What are the objectives of any of our courses? If the objectives are not to replicate the disciplines, then how can pedagogical structures be achieved which will permit the topical and hopefully flexible use of knowledge while offering the logical continuity in studies that the powerful organization of the subject design yields?

To begin with, a social studies course must recognize its nature. The social education of citizens is an applied field—not a scientific one per se. It involves applying information to social problems and using cogent, intellectual processes in the resolution of these problems. The effective utilization of knowledge includes that derived from the realm of feeling, the realm of science, and the realm of heterogeneous knowing. Intelligent, skillful teaching in the social studies would mean giving due respect to each of these realms rather than placing the full burden on the social science disciplines, asking of them what they were not intended to give.

A social studies course should not be expected to achieve specific, measurable objectives in the scientific sense, for it is not strictly a scientific course; it must become involved in the affective acting of citizens. Insofar as it delves into the affective, it escapes accurate quantitative measurement and is best represented by qualitative description. That is, we cannot say that the citizen should be honest to the tenth degree or that a "good" citizen abides by all or even most of the laws of his country. The laws must be put in a context—as must such descriptions as "good" or "honest." The laws of gravity affect all the earth's stones in a consistent, repeatable fashion that allows the assignment of a specific "quantity." The laws of men are dependent on varying situations. The unique experiences and situations of men are repeatable in only grossest fashion. The Italian peasant who was milked dry by his Bourbon ruler and who turned to the Mafia for help and protection might well have been as honest as the American worker who turns to his labor union. But even if it were ascertained that both the peasant and the worker were "honest," the equality of their "honesty" would be impossible to prove. The input to attain honesty would be so profoundly diverse that there would be little basis for exact comparison. The situational elements of human behavior are so many and so varied that no scheme has yet been attained which permits measurable comparison through time, or between separate cultures, or even between groups of people within the same society. In formulating the objectives of a social studies course, it must be realized that only very general, encompassing objectives can be achieved. The specific behavioral objective, which has become so popular in recent times, could never adequately represent the scope and breadth of a course in social education.

Recognizing the necessary imprecision of social studies objectives in no way means that there should be no objectives. The comparison of intended goals and actual achievements is a necessary, if not sufficient, measure of the success of any educational undertaking. Are the desired outcomes too distant from the actual achievement?

The awareness of goals also permits an evaluation of the desired goals in education within the context of what is societally desirable. For example, knowing that one of the primary goals of education is "Americanization," no matter how vague the meaning may be, permits an evaluation with regard to whether "Americanization" is being achieved by the educational system. American historians are generally agreed that our system of mass education has greatly contributed to the Americanization of the immigrant. They would, however, be hard pressed to achieve agreement regarding a set of characteristics that would describe the American. Further, being aware of the goal to Americanize permits an analysis concerning whether that goal continues to be compatible with those goals accepted as societally desirable. The goal does not have to be in specific terms to be useful. In the case of "Americanization," the concept of a "standard American" may be in the process of becoming less desirable societally.

2 Decision Making:
The Focus of Social Education

Now that we see that the objectives will be quite general, the sources of these objectives must nevertheless be determined. If social studies is to be focused on citizenship education, then clearly we must concentrate upon the essence of citizenship. The heart of citizenship is decision making Whatever his state of preparation, the citizen is called upon to make a myriad of decisions. These decisions may concern societal goals and the means of their attainment or they may concern his own personal behavior regarding these goals. He makes his decisions on the basis of his conceptions of what is possible and what is best. His conception of what is possible may be thought of as descriptive or explanatory of the relationships among the realities that he perceives in the world around him. They may be considered descriptive models or pictures in the mind's eye of how sets of circumstances are, in fact, causally related. His conceptions of what is best are value oriented and may be considered prescriptive models of how sets of circumstances ought to be related. The first kind of model is a summary of one's facts. It is the business of social science and history to clarify and create such models. The second is a summary of one's values. It is the business of philosophy to clarify and create these models. The vital interaction of both as the foundation of decision making is the business of social studies.

Quite aside from any educational effort, the citizen is a model maker. The various conceptions which he brings to his decision making are correctly thought of as models, each one of which summarizes in his mind some segment of his knowledge or experience. Thus, he may conceive of how economic matters are or ought to be handled in his society. He may conceive of how a life is or ought to be lived. He arranges his models into systems, that is, within his general economics model he may conceive of how indebtedness is handled and how it ought to be handled. The life that is or ought to be includes how one does or ought to treat his pal or his girl friend, and the like. A particular student on a particular day carries a complete picture of society, which, however inaccurate and limited, nonetheless, he uses to explain any situation which he may meet. This is the structure upon which new learning is most easily built.

To the extent that he has stopped to think about it, the various subsystems that make up the overarching models each individual carries in his mind may be consistent with one another. However, individuals are fully capable of harboring many inconsistent models of reality and conflicting conceptions of what is good or what ought to be. Thus, one of the major goals of civic education should be to help the individual develop more accurate, comprehensive, and consistent models upon which to base his behavior.

In a very real sense, education is what stays in our mind after the specifics of what we have learned have been forgotten. We forget the details but we remember the impression which the details made upon us. We forget the facts. The generalizations we draw from them can hardly be forgotten. The cloth of models is woven from generalizations. Models are systems or patterns drawn from man's perceptions of existence. Existence itself may be considered theoretical or real or on a continuum of both. Education may help us realize more powerful models, that is, models which give us control over more, and more varied situations. The extent of our capacity to cope with new situations will depend on the quality of the models available to the mind.

Generalizing, theorizing, and modeling are natural human proclivities. We do it so smoothly and easily that many of us are unaware of the impressions and bases by which we chart our lives. The job of education is to bring the model-making process out into the open and to improve the quality of the models which we use in interpreting new situations in the environment. This clearly is not merely a matter of imparting more and more information to be used later, but rather a matter of utilizing information in the process of modifying one's models and reaching decisions.

Models are not only the mechanisms of utilizing learning, but are also the mechanisms of extending learning to new areas of experience. Just as the scholar brings to his study some theory or model of how he thinks affairs are organized and uses a model to guide his investigation until such time as it is shown to be incorrect or incomplete, so the student learns most when his model is challenged by conflicting data which cannot be made to fit the model, or by the presentation of another model which more accurately and completely summarizes and explains a set of data. The confrontation of existing models should be a central part of social studies. In this way, the student's attitude and approach to his own models can be led toward greater flexibility and willingness to change.

In concentrating on decision making, we have noted that the objectives of a course in social studies should be the development of models within the individual which are more *consistent*, more *powerful*, more *consciously held*, and more *flexible* than would have been true without a course in social studies. It is hoped that students will become more qualified citizens, that is, better able to make decisions because of their citizen education studies.

Within the context of citizenship education, the manner in which models will be made more consistent, powerful, conscious, and flexible will depend largely on the quality of government underlying citizenship. If the form of government that is dominant is totalitarian, "consistent" will mean that the citizen's models fall into a pattern that is increasingly logical within the dictates of the regime; "powerful" will refer to the citizen's ability to apply the principles of the regime with greater acuity; "conscious" will stress the awareness of patriotism; "flexible" will mean the ability of the citizen to modify his models according to the changes made by the government. Although in his personal relationships the individual may be involved in vital decision making, as a citizen the quality of his decision making is insignificant, being secondary to that of the totalitarian regime. He is a receptor of rather than a participant in government.

If the form of government is democratic, the citizen's

decision making becomes central to the government's functioning. "Consistent," then, could mean a continual evaluation of public decisions on the part of the individual citizen to see whether the goals and morals which the citizen holds as desirable are sustained; "powerful" could refer to the citizen's ability to improve the models of government; "conscious" could represent a striving for more complete and independent understanding of society by the citizen; "flexible" could mean not only the willingness to accept new models, but the desire to search for models better than those in use by the government.

In a democratic nation, it is logical to assume that a course in citizenship education will focus on significant decision making. That is, although the actual laws and structures of a society may be studied, the objective of that study will be primarily not one of obedience but rather one of active participation. The citizen is first a law maker and only then does he become law abiding.

If social studies is to be a course in democratic citizenship education, it must acknowledge that students are already citizens. Students do not lose their citizenship because they are students. They will learn what quality of decision making is desirable and/or possible not only from the content presented, but from the very way the course is organized.

Thus, we have said that the objectives of social studies in a democracy should be directed toward increasing significant decision-making abilities as opposed to insignificant decision-making abilities consonant with totalitarianism. In a democracy the citizen is thought of as being in control of his government rather than being subject to it. We have further said that the student must be accepted as a significant decision maker when he enters the social studies course. The increasing of his decision-making abilities so that they become more consistent, powerful, conscious, and flexible should be based on the models he bears when he begins his study of citizenship education. In a democratic society, we must treat the young as significant decision makers whose models can be and hopefully will be improved.

The analysis of objectives takes us one step further. We must ask what are the characteristics of a good citizen in a democratic society? If his decisions are to contribute to the improvement of government, he must be adept in making generalizations for the government must operate from generalizations. Information must lead to understanding and to meaningful models concerning societal relationships. The citizen must be able to move from particular events to overall conceptions. He may never know all the facts, but he must base his models for decision upon those facts he has. If he were to wait for all the facts, he might never put his decision-making function into operation. At the same time, he must be prepared to modify his models when the presentation of new information or more accurate models makes this worthwhile. Indeed, he must actively seek new knowledge and new models if he is to participate in the improvement of his government. Thus, while he is generalizing, he must also be willing to suspend judgment; while he is deciding, he must also be speculating. Much more information than he can ever remember should be available, or should at least be sought.

The citizen should be aware of the quality of his decisions. He should be conscious of the reliability of his information, as well as of his model. He should be aware of the relative importance that his decisions carry so that he will not be sidetracked with insignificant issues, while major problems are resolved by a handful of men. A complex, democratic government will necessarily represent a meshing of decisions only some of which will be of major importance. He should be conscious of how he is applying his values to the decisions he makes. He should be constantly comparing his value systems with those fostered by his government.

With this conception of a significant decision maker and with the recognition that the student is already a citizen bearing his own models when he enters a social studies course, it becomes clear that teaching must be the act of confronting the student with situations that will lead him to reconsider the models of his environment, as well as his way of perceiving them. The end of learning is more accurate, comprehensive, and useful structuring in the mind of the individual student.

3 The Sources of Decision-Making Models

It is important to recognize the extent to which the citizen's models come from sources lying outside formal education. While there is no way of knowing the extent, it is obvious that today's citizen gets the bulk of his beliefs outside the classroom. Knowledge gained in the home and on the street has a tremendous advantage over formal education in that it is usually immediately relevant to something the learner wants to know and, therefore, is more easily assimilated into the mind. One lesson on the street is worth several lessons in a classroom atmosphere. Despite our frequent lament about how poorly students master what is taught in history, government, geography, etc., it is obvious that these same students do learn more outside the classroom. They master a social system complete with its own history, sociology, economics, and values. Students may come to social studies with many erroneous and poorly founded beliefs, but they do not come with empty heads.

What are the various sources for the citizen's models that contribute to the decisions he makes? This is a question vital to the determination of relevant social studies. Some of these sources, by no means mutually exclusive categories but nevertheless representative of different dimensions in the formulation of the citizen's models, follow.

1. *The citizen gets both descriptive and prescriptive models from the vague, subverbal impressions that arise out of his conglomerate experiences.* These models may be formed almost as by osmosis; that is, soaked up from peers, elders, and teachers through overt behavior, by ·gesture, by connotation, or expression. In short, the citizen has probably done very little solid thinking about these models. The role of social studies is to help him accomplish continual, cogent reformulation of his own thinking within the realm of his experiences. It is to make his models more consistent and conscious within a context that he can understand.

Not to be underestimated among these heterogeneous sources of the citizen's models is his life in the school. The school is the one institution in which all young citizens spend the greatest portion of their waking hours. The general nature and tone of life in the school, the way power is exercised, the way rewards and punishments are allocated, the attitudes displayed toward intelligent behavior both inside and outside the classroom—all of these and a myriad of other matters experienced in school are more powerful in the formation of models than are the abstract and highly verbal experiences constituting the formal content of learning in the classroom.

2. *The citizen gets models from exemplars presented in the aesthetic production of the world around him.* The world of art, music, literature, the theatre, television, and so forth, are continually presenting forceful exemplars of behavior. The influence of these media on model formation rivals—if it does not surpass—that of formal education in the school. Some are enlightened and serious efforts to deal with man's condition. It is too much to expect, however, that students will meet only the good exemplars in life, avoiding the bad. Deliberate propaganda, insincere and prurient art and literature, extremism, selfish motives, deliberate falsehood, semantic trickery, hypocrisy, and misleading advertising can all be expected to play a part in forming the character of the citizen. The point here is that if values are the touchstone of decision making—and a separation of these in our daily lives is incomprehensible—it is quite as important to help citizens build defenses against such intellectual and aesthetic trickery as it is to expose them to the so-called "good" values (herein defined as serious and enlightened efforts to deal honestly with man's condition). Skill in discriminating between the serious and the exploitive elements among exemplars and in ferreting out the good from the dross cannot be ignored as part of social studies education. Thus, such matters as semantics and art criticism among others become rightfully part of social education.

3. *The citizen gets prescriptive models from the religion, philosophy, and traditional beliefs of his culture.* People have ideas not only about how reality actually is, but also about how it ought to be. These valuations play the dominant role in decision making. The citizen's basic value models are likely to rest on the religious and philosophic ideas embraced by his culture and learned at his mother's knee. The traditional ways of believing and be-

having in the culture—the folkways—may be accepted by the individual without question. Value models which are internally inconsistent and at variance with facts may be treated as if they were fact and all of one piece.

Human beings never suffer from a lack of values. Rather they may harbor many unexamined values which are inconsistent with one another, or which have been developed in ignorance of viable alternatives. An important role of the social studies is that of helping the student to examine his value models and to broaden his value base with a consequent increasing of the viable alternatives from which he may choose. This means the study of values and of value problems must become a central concern, rather than the stepchild of the social studies endeavor. Implicitly, this could be conceived as involving the systematic effort to identify and classify the values operative in the culture; the comparative study of values between parent cultures or between subcultures within parent cultures; the continual focus on the value problems in decisions which citizens are called upon to make; the confrontation of students with the inconsistencies which exist among our individual and societal values; the formal study and practice of the strategies involved in resolving value conflict; and the provision of opportunities for honest and frank discourse to continually take place among students and teachers over matters of value.

4. *The citizen gets descriptive models of reality from the social sciences.* The social sciences afford basic theoretical models of human behavior as it is or is thought to be. The social sciences do not provide models of how man ought to be, that is, they do not provide prescriptive models. The social sciences are not basically concerned with charting trends or sociocultural drift. This is the business of history. The method of the social sciences is that of cross-sectional analysis. Each social science in-

quires into the relationships that exist in a field of human activity at a fixed time in history or generally over all time.

Thus the building of analytical models is the particular job of the social sciences. Models of human behavior are provided by the sciences of economics, sociology, psychology, political science, etc. Each attempts to describe, account for and even predict the behavior of men with respect to some limited aspect of human behavior; that is, economics is concerned with economic behavior as a pure phenomenon standing alone from other behavior, sociology is concerned with groups, psychology with the individual, and so forth.

To the degree that the model is accurate or true (no model presently known in the social sciences is more than an approximation), we may venture to predict how a society will behave now or in the future and we may suggest the avenues open for its development. But we should be warned that social sciences models are gross, theoretical instruments liable to grave inaccuracies; mankind frequently opts to control his own affairs and change the direction of his development. Thus, history bears a reciprocal relationship to the social sciences in that it focuses on change in the whole system which the social sciences are trying piecemeal to analyze and describe.

Further, no social science standing alone is capable of describing or explaining a particular human act or of telling how to behave in a particular situation. Each social science, as Pendelton Herring[1] has said, can limit the scope of guessing and uninformed speculation, but this fact does not in and of itself solve the problem.

[1]Pendelton Herring, "Toward an Understanding of Man," in Roy A. Price (ed.), *New Viewpoints in the Social Sciences*, Twenty-eighth Yearbook, Washington, D.C.: National Council for the Social Studies, 1958, pp. 1–19.

An economic solution of a problem on the actual human scene may not be a viable solution because there are sociological, political, or humanitarian factors which must also be considered. Thus the decision to maintain full employment in our society is not a responsibility for economists to take, and to talk about such a matter is outside the pale of economics, but the economic model does have a useful bearing on the problem which should not be ignored by any intelligent citizen.

Above all, it should be underlined that there is no certain knowledge in any social science field. As a matter of fact, each of the social sciences is today undergoing profound modification involving such basic questions as that of the very parameters of the field. For instance, political scientists today are sharply divided between the traditionalists (or legalists), the activists (or reformers), and the behaviorists over the question, What is political science?

Therefore, to teach the current findings of social science scholarship without awareness of the state of these disciplines and the approach which each takes to knowledge is really to perpetrate a cruel hoax and to foist off erroneous and oversure models on the student. Instead, the student should be taken into the confidence of the scholar. He must be given full knowledge of the problems which confront the scholars in each field.

If he is really to be the master of the analytical models which the social sciences afford, the student must be permitted to master the analytical methodology by which the scholar comes to have dependable knowledge. If these models are to have any significance for the citizen's function as a decision maker, he should be allowed and encouraged to collect and handle actual data and construct his own homemade models. These homemade models could then be fruitfully compared to the more sophisticated models of the scholar. The role of social studies would be to offer the bridges necessary for such comparisons.

5. *The citizen gets developmental or temporal models from history.* From historical accounts, one gets models of change, development, trend and direction, or what some call a sense of sociocultural drift. It is impossible for the individual to understand or interpret his own experience without first locating himself in history—although, for this purpose, a mythological history could serve as well as more objective history. In the latter sense history becomes a kind of backward projection of our behavior with possible therapeutic values.

But if history is to provide models of sociocultural drift, it must be fairly comprehensive history more or less in the grand style of McNeil, Toynbee, Spengler, Muller, and others. A focus on recording and remembering details and fragments of history without thought for the grand design will hardly do the trick. Instead, a fairly high degree of generalization is necessary before history yields its story. Outright speculation is not only permissible but frequently highly productive of models. Historical thinking has always had its artistic and humanistic components alongside its cannons of objectivities.

Within the context and purposes of social studies, this comprehensive treatment of history may vary in scope. Suitable rubrics would include: man in the cosmos, and the development over all time of *human* cultures, institutions, and technologies. Somewhat lesser histories are needed to give perspective to contemporary developments and ideologies, e.g., industrialization, nationalism, democracy, the welfare society, internationalism, and the like. In a similar vein, histories are needed to place in perspective the persistent high-level problems and ideological conflicts in world society, including, among others, problems of continuity and change in human society; changing human goals and institutional redevelopment; population and food; technology and full employment; the struggle for freedom and individual integrity; technological change and moral breakdown; and coping with cultural and ideological differences.

Ironically, we have typically organized the study of history along such localistic lines and toward such limited objectives that we have managed to destroy much of its usefulness in model building. We have persistently ignored the problem of immediate relevance and even now we continue to teach history that is no longer viable while contemporary problems of first importance are neglected. History teaching is infamous for never getting to the present. We forever put off the day when students are encouraged to generalize from historical data, thus robbing them of the opportunity to really get the point of history. It is an opportunity that the social studies must provide, for the seeking and studying of new models, new alternatives for the citizen, is the major business of social studies.

Further, the citizen should be taken into the fold of the historians just as we suggested earlier he must be taken into the fold of the social scientists. The citizen must be led to make their problems his problems, their tools his tools. There has never yet existed a version of history that has entirely withstood the onslaught of its critics. Witness what Vann Woodward and Strydon are doing to the history of slavery and reconstruction. As change comes about, we ask new questions of history. The citizen must learn to ask these questions and it is the role of the social studies to help him do so.

6. *The citizen gets analytical models from established systems of logical thought found in philosophy, logic, and mathematics.* The citizen need not have studied mathematics, logic, or philosophy in depth to use the analytic models which have been developed by these disciplines. Formal models of analysis pervade our entire culture.

It is not necessary for the citizen to realize that he is thinking deductively, inductively, or retroductively. It is not necessary for him to be able to distinguish the types of logical fallacies by name. The fact is he uses these models continually even if he does so unconsciously. Every time he concludes from three or four cases of political corruption that all politicians are corrupt, he is following a model (even if somewhat inadequate) for inductive thought. Whenever he recognizes that criticizing the organization and administration of a school is fundamentally different from criticizing an individual teacher, he is operating with an analytical model of logical fallacy.

There is a natural proclivity in man to use analytical models. Some of his models for logical thought he has achieved on his own; some have come to him, more or less unconsciously, as cultural heritages; some he has learned from the formal disciplines. In confronting a social situation he may be unaware of the logical models he is using. He may even engage simultaneously in logical and illogical mental operations without realizing his inconsistencies. It is one of the functions of education to bring formal analysis into the open so that the student may become more aware and more able to cope with his logical models. Such awareness may be achieved in two related ways: through the formal study of logic, philosophy, and math, and through the analysis of those thought processes which the individual uses in interpreting his own experiences. If the social studies are to improve the decision-making abilities of citizens, logical analyses must be dealt with as a part of the citizen's development. Social studies can contribute to the improved use of logical models in everyday life by underscoring how they are used, how they could be used, and the limits of their use.

7. *The citizen gets both descriptive and prescriptive*

models heuristically when the need to act on either a small or grand scale confronts him. In resolving a real life problem, the individual is required in some way to fit together or synthesize all of the contributing models that he has somehow acquired. In this process each of the contributing models is to some extent modified and meshed together with other models. A new overarching model takes shape which thereafter is used to deal in a general way with a general kind or class of problem.

Thus, out of the confrontation with a particular problem in the area of conservation as, for instance, air and water pollution, we may develop a general model for dealing with such a class of problems. The ready existence of such general models in the minds of people is everywhere evident. Men can even be classified as generally conservative or generally liberal, and the like, on the basis of the general working models to which they continually refer problems in the society. Such models have only a loose relationship, if any relationship at all, to possible component models in historical, economic, political, sociological, or philosophical understanding. General model building is a matter of working out an accommodation among the component models *of which one is aware*, thus freeing oneself to act.

The confrontation with a social problem and particularly the need to act is, therefore, an important catalyst for model formation. Out of such confrontation general ways for dealing with social situations take form, becoming the overarching models for action. The responsibility of the school is to advance the quality of these general models, just as it is to advance the quality of the more limited models growing out of the study of subjects in the curriculum. If the education of citizens is the concern of social studies, then the improvement in the general models to which citizens refer their problems, should also be the concern of social studies. This involves helping citizens to gain a greater awareness of the full gamut of component models. It also involves helping citizens to develop better intellectual techniques for thinking about social problems. There *are* better intellectual and social strategies for dealing with broad social problems than most citizens possess. To learn these ways, the process of model formation in broad social situations must become an explicit subject of study, its parts must be identified and refined through analysis, and experience must be gained in using these better procedures. Contributing to such improvements are techniques for the better definition of a problem; techniques for judging the pertinency of various models to a given problem; techniques involved in discovering how others feel about the problem and why others may feel differently than oneself; and techniques involved in the resolution of problems through political action.

4 Toward a Logically Powerful Topical Design

THE NEED FOR LOGICAL POWER IN TOPICAL ORGANIZATION

Seven major sources of the models that citizens bear with them have just been discussed. In brief review, these are models arising out of the conglomerate of vague, sub-verbal impressions; models arising from exemplars; models arising from the religion, philosophy, and traditional beliefs of the culture; models arising from the social sciences; models arising from history; models of formal analysis; and models arising from the need to act. Throughout the discussion of these categories, their pertinence in determining the input of a social studies course has been emphasized.

Nonetheless, it must be recognized that these sources

are neither mutually exclusive nor similar in type. There is considerable overlapping and interaction, just as there is overlapping and interaction in our real life models. For curriculum construction, the direct use of these categories would mean a logically weak structure. Logical ordering is a means of increasing man's intellectual power and control over his environment. Until now, it has been his most successful means. The school's efforts have always been toward preparing the young so that they may face their environment more successfully. Logical structure is an important contribution to this preparation. While the sources presented are quite valid for the formulation of social studies topics, i.e., specific content input, they do not offer the social studies a powerful means of overall content organization.

To some considerable extent, the problem of content organization in the social studies parallels the problem of content organization in every area of the educational endeavor. While topics offer an interdisciplinary means for getting at the specific problems of our times, there is a crying need for an overall structure that will bring the strength of logical ordering to the topical approach. Although recognizing the increased personal relevancy possible with the use of current topics, social studies followed the entire field of education in the late 1950s and 1960s, reverting to a discipline orientation. The need for a curriculum structure more powerful than any that has been derived from the Progressive movement was made urgent under the Sputnik push. It was felt that a revision of the pedagogical structure of subjects, along with the adoption of new teaching methodologies could revitalize the scholastic content based on the disciplines.

Yet, the gap between student interests and scholastic concerns has continued to widen. The belief that the schools are irrelevant has continued to grow. The failure of the schools to achieve personal relevancy has led many to believe that even the societally relevant studies undertaken by the schools are irrelevant.

In the social studies, the struggle has been between societal and personal relevancy. On the one hand, a topical input involving the student's experiences seems the primary means of achieving relevancy for citizenship education; on the other hand, the logical weaknesses of topical ordering turn the educator back to more powerful instruments of curriculum construction. The sources of the citizen's models, as we have seen, are not logically ordered. The gap between student concerns and educational concerns widens and it is up to the educator to find a solution. The development of curriculum which would permit a topical input while ordering this input in some logically powerful way is clearly the next step.

THE OPEN CURRICULUM STRUCTURE: THE ACHIEVEMENT OF PERSONAL AND SOCIETAL RELEVANCY

Before attempting to develop a logically powerful topical design, a major distinction must be made between a *closed curriculum structure* and an *open curriculum structure*. The great flexibility of the subject curriculum must be recognized in this regard. While subjects do closely reflect the disciplines, the choice of disciplines may vary, thus permitting a continual change in the emphasis and direction of study. For example, between 1860 and 1920 subjects such as Greek, Latin, surveying, and declamation were dropped from the average secondary school program while modern foreign languages, economics, American history, and music were added. Furthermore, in the comprehensive American high school it is possible for the student to select from an array of subjects. This possibility of selection gives the illusion that personal as well as societal relevancy is being achieved by means of the subject curriculum. In reality, once the subjects are chosen, the models they present deal with isolated phenomena. All else is held suspended while the particular models of a particular discipline are worked with. Not dealt with are the interactions of models derived from various disciplines as well as from no particular discipline occurring in the individual's daily life. The inability of the subject-based curriculum to deal with such pressing problems as student unrest on campus, the rising drop-out rate, the increasing drug addiction among the young, pollution, poverty, and urbanization, has underscored the inadequacies of this type of curriculum despite its apparent flexibility and its logical structuring of content.

The subject design, notwithstanding its flexibility with regard to the disciplines chosen, offers a closed curriculum structure. If one does not study or "do" physics in a physics course or biology in a biology course, then clearly the disciplines are being disregarded and the curriculum design employed is not a subject-oriented one. The purpose of a subject is to make the content and structure of a discipline pedagogically manageable. If the basic nature of the discipline is changed, then the subject is not following its purpose.

An open curriculum structure would offer an underlying logic of organization which would not be dependent on a specific content input. For example, if the uses of hypothesizing are to be studied, the scientific hypothesis could become the specific content input, but not necessarily. Literary hypotheses or the use of hypothesizing in the understanding of practical situations could also serve as specific content input. Indeed, the specific content could be manipulated and changed in what might be an infinite number of ways without jeopardizing the logical structure. Even when a specific topic such as scientific hypothesizing is selected, the choice of input and treatment remains vast. The teacher may wish to base his selection on the students' direct experiences and may choose the sequential development of a boy into manhood. Or, he may turn to less personal experiences, choosing the question of how bodies float in air and water. In any event, he could be teaching his students the significance of scientific hypothesizing. The open curriculum structure, then, would permit a wide range of differing types of content even while the logic and goals of the overall design are being achieved.

The distinction between the closed curriculum structure and the open curriculum structure helps clarify the fact that "flexibility" within the educational discourse does not automatically signify personal relevancy. We have already noted the flexibility of the subject curriculum, i.e., its ability to delete disciplines, to add new disciplines and to offer a range of studies for selection by the individual student. Notwithstanding this flexibility, the subject curriculum is usually not personally relevant to the student; it has not succeeded in making the student feel that what he is studying is vital to his life. The closed curriculum structure, which must accompany the subject design, is an important factor in this irrelevancy. The content input of a subject must follow certain principles. The strength of a discipline lies in the tight logical cohesion of its underlying principles. As we have already stated, these principles are assumed to operate while all else stands still. What could be more irrelevant to the models of daily existence? The ongoing action and interaction of established models and of models in the process of formulation can only be revealed in a topical approach.

The open curriculum structure achieves flexibility through a wide range of heterogeneous content selections. Furthermore, once the content to be dealt with has been chosen, it must be treated in an open-ended fashion. The answers must not have been predetermined; the alternatives must not have been limited in number or type. While the flexible choice of topics is essential to the achievement of increased personal relevancy, the advantage gained from flexible content input is lost unless the content is used in such a way that changing conclusions and alternative courses of action may arise in the minds of students. Such open-endedness requires that the teacher himself recognize that he does not have all the right answers. The underlying assumption is that man is still in search of truth. Whether there is or is not absolute truth, every individual has the right to look for it as best he can.

Two sources of curriculum flexibility have been discussed. One arises as a function of the curriculum structure. The other occurs through the open-ended treatment of the content itself. Both types of curriculum flexibility, taken together, require a topical design and are not attainable through the subject design.

THE USE OF TOPICS AND MEDIA TO INCREASE FLEXIBILITY AND PERSONAL RELEVANCY

It has been indicated above that the topical approach to curriculum and the open-ended treatment of the content by the teacher are major sources for obtaining flexibility and personal relevance in the open curriculum structure. The elaboration of topical flexibility may be achieved through the continuous modification of topics. That is, new points for discussion may be sought which will contribute to the guiding objective. For example, in the study of human relations, the topic of "Marriage" could be substituted for the topic of "Resistance to Middle-Class Family Life" and this in turn by the topic of "Sex Without Love." In the study of ecology, "Industrial Pollution" could be substituted for "Population Control" or "Urbanization." Even when the topics do not change, they may be expanded or somehow given a new twist. The topic of "Marriage" may be retained in a some-what challenging fashion, for example, "Marriage: Do We Know What It Is?" Such changes are consonant with an open curriculum structure. Topics may be posed as prob-lems. The very search for problems may become a topic of study. Improved tools of research may be sought. Manipulations of this nature are based on an open-ended conception of the content itself once it has been chosen.

The further elaboration of the open-ended treatment of content involves the way the content is presented. Until fairly recently, the primary pedagogical instrument uti-lized in the schools was the written word. This is chang-ing. The young are involved in manipulating media which are equally as powerful as the written word (if not more so) even before they reach school age. The radio, televi-sion, movies, cassettes, and recordings along with a host of electronic machines have introduced new means of expressing and reaching understanding. McLuhan has already recognized the importance of these various media as carriers of meaning. In saying that the media are all that count, McLuhan may have underestimated the power of meaning or the semantic input. However, he has rec-ognized that the syntax or structure imposed by one or another medium is significant to how we think about our meanings. A stone statue of a man excites a conceptually different approach in us from that of an oil painting of a man. When we view the statue, we somehow want to walk around behind the figure; we want to touch it, per-haps even feel the strength of the stone; the only space that counts is the space that is hammered out of the air by the stone of the statue. A painting would inhibit our desire to survey the figure completely; it would force us to imagine innumerable details; its space is well defined by the canvas and two-dimensional props employed by the painter and, if anything, we must relate the painted space to our own conceptions of space. The semantic input, which is the man, remains unchanged, but the way we think of the man changes with the syntactical ordering or structure imposed by a given media.

Within the pedagogical discourse, the concept of media as a way of reinterpreting topics must be extended to include teaching approaches. The way materials are presented in the educational setting represents pedagogical media, which extend well beyond the media developed by technology. The teacher may make a startling statement at the beginning of class. He may follow this up with a highly dramatic film which leaves unanswered questions. He may then give a list of research topics related to the film and his statement. These are his pedagogical media.

In brief review, curriculum flexibility has been related to ways of treating topics so that they are in a continuous state of change. One of these involves manipulating or changing the semantic input of the topics (e.g., "Marriage" into "Marriage: Do We Know What It Is?"). The second does not deal with the topics themselves, but with the media used to present the topics. A different view of the same topic can be achieved by use of different media. The view of media has been, furthermore, expanded to include both the technological media and teaching techniques. This expanded conception has been called pedagogical media.

Decisions concerning what pedagogical media should be chosen for a specific topic are made on at least two levels. The curriculum developer of materials chooses the technological media to be used. He may also give suggestions for teaching activities. However, his position in relation to the actual classroom situation is necessarily a distant one. He works according to general sequential principles, and laws of averages. The teacher, on the other hand, will make decisions concerning the pedagogical media which are of an immediate nature, based on the group personality of his class, their needs and capacities,

and his own personality. This means that the media
determined by the curriculum developer must be so
created that the teacher will have a wide margin within
which to operate.

While the semantic manipulations of topics may be
derived from the sources of decision-making models,
some of which have already been discussed, the manipulation of topics through the pedagogical media does not fit
into these sources. It is another dimension in teaching
which does modify the student's conceptual approach. If
a student has made his primary gains in learning through
pictures and television, relevancy to his way of learning
can be achieved by making use of these media. Moreover,
by making use of a variety of media, it becomes possible
to extend the student's experiences in the media and in
the thought patterns that each one establishes. The manipulation of pedagogical media can ensure increased
student involvement.

AN OVERVIEW OF THE THREE PHASES
COMPRISING CURRICULUM DEVELOPMENT

Curriculum development clearly involves more than a
design for organizing content. The pedagogical media to
be used and the sources for valid content are factors vital
to scholastic success. The media, the content sources and
the curriculum design must all abide by certain criteria
if one is not to annul the effects of the other. The total
curriculum complex must be logically powerful, open-
structured, flexible and personally relevant, i.e., the
process of content selection must permit wide variation
as well as logical sequencing, the choice of media must
be flexible while congruency with the teaching objectives
is maintained.

In a very general fashion, the three phases of curriculum development have been dealt with. A diagram of the

different elements perceived as contributing to a successful social studies course follows.

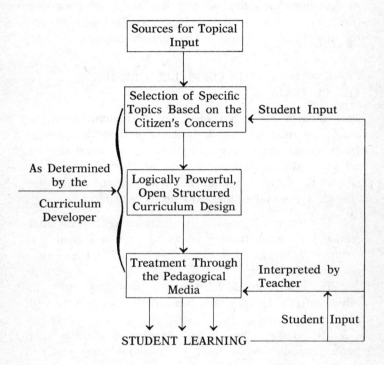

This simple diagram represents the cumulative effects of curriculum structuring. Topic selection or the content to be studied is subject to manipulation in and of itself. Once the parameters of a topic have been defined, the topic undergoes further manipulation first through the curriculum design and then by means of pedagogical media, to which both the curriculum designer, the teacher, and the students contribute. The process of preparing materials for the teaching stage is not complete until both content selection and media selection have been related to a curriculum design which will give the student a sense of consistency in what he studies so that his ability to deal with his models will increase through the development of logical control and through the discernment of overarching generalizations.

ZEROING IN ON THE CURRICULUM DESIGN: THE CRITERIA

The construction of an adequate curriculum design requires an awareness of the criteria guiding that design. In exploring the nature and goals of the social studies, we have already indicated some of the criteria which should guide the development of a valid curriculum design for the social studies. Among these criteria are:

1. The design should deal with its content in an intellectually rigorous fashion so as to yield a logical consistency at least as powerful as that yielded by the subject curriculum.

2. The design should ensure more immediate, individually oriented relevancy than is presently achieved through the subject curriculum.

3. The design should be capable of dealing with heterogeneous topical input, i.e., it should have an open curriculum structure based on the full range of sources.

4. The design should encourage open-ended treatment of specific content selection.

As we zero in on the development of the curriculum design, other criteria come to mind. The construction of a curriculum design for the social studies should represent the content that will be studied. A tightly logical design for the study of geography misses the point if one must know economics. This example is, of course, an exaggeration, but it brings home its point. No matter how finely woven a curriculum design is, if it is not suited to the objectives, if it does not deal with what must be dealt with, then it has missed the point. If the purpose of a social studies course is to teach significant decision making, then to concentrate on the structures of government and the obedience owed these is to miss the point. We must base our design on the sources for the citizen's decision making models. As we have noted, these sources are no more than a potpourri of the ways a citizen obtains his models. For the most part, they have no logical thread uniting them. The question then is to find this logical thread among the sources and make it a part of the curriculum design.

The citizen's decision-making models have their origins in the personal world of the citizen as well as in the greater society about him. Both these origins should be carefully attended to. If either is emphasized to the neglect of the other, citizenship cannot be fully dealt with. A valid curriculum design for the social studies must develop those sources whose origins are primarily of a personal nature as well as those whose origins are primarily of a societal nature. The design should provide for a content capable of dealing simultaneously with personal and societal concerns.

The personal and societal exist in a scalar relationship in which one may say that something is more or less personal, more or less societal. For instance, a topic such as "Man and Freedom" may shift positions between the personal and the societal according to the pedagogical treatment and the particular focus. Other topics cannot be moved so easily along the scale without extending the content areas being referred to. For instance, "Bureaucracy" and "Industrialization" are topics primarily based upon a societal context. While the individual may experience them personally, they are inconceivable without large masses.

Considering the content of what is to be studied leads us to still another criterion. The curriculum design should tap all the conceivable sources for the models. Consistency in reasoning, which is fundamental to logic, does not necessarily imply completeness unless the parameters of completeness and the intention to reach these are stipulated. Because a K–12 social studies program would have as its objectives a citizen familiar with and able to function in all conceivable models of significant decision making, completeness becomes a vital criterion for the curriculum design. In this work, seven sources have been discussed. There are, no doubt, others awaiting discernment and discussion.

The criterion of tapping all sources leads us back to the problem of the knowledge explosion. Whatever else the schools may do, they must help the young to cope with the enormity of information that is now threatening to overwhelm them. The priority must be toward generalization not specialization, toward principles of better living not principles merely good for the production of more technological advances. Thus, the design should encourage the development of the individual's ability to handle information and to generalize.

Helping the student to cope with the explosion of knowledge means involving him in the improvement of his own models, encouraging him to seek new models, and so forth. The curriculum plan should make it necessary to involve the student not only in meaningful verbal learning, but in problem solving and discovery. The when, the how, and the quantity of student involvement can best be made on the basis of knowledge concerning the particular class composition, the teacher's own personality, and the materials to be dealt with. While the curriculum plan may avoid specific decisions for student involvement, it should present the means of student involvement.

In brief review, five criteria have been added to the first list. These are:

1. The design should be based on the sources for the citizen's decision-making models.

2. The design should provide for a balanced treatment of the personal and the societal in the sources.

3. The design should afford completeness, i.e., tap all the sources of the citizen's models.

4. The design should encourage students to generalize, and thus increase their ability to cope with the increasing quantity of knowledge.

5. The design should ensure active student involvement.

5 Action-Concepts: The Basis for a New Curriculum Design

Because a major objective of our design revolves around personal relevancy, we felt that this concern must be built into the design itself. This could be achieved either by making a division between the personal and the societal, or by finding classifications which, by their nature, could afford both personal and societal input. The former possibility seemed to lead to a series of arbitrary distinctions between the personal and the societal bearing very little relationship to life. Furthermore, it would lead to a new kind of fragmentation, a defect of the discipline-oriented curriculum which we were hoping to escape. Therefore, a range of concepts were sought that would be equally valid in dealing with personal and societal experiences.

In seeking such concepts, we came to realize that a major distinction had to be made between concepts descriptive of institutions and individuals, and concepts describing actions. Static descriptions of societal establishments are likely to be radically different from any to be found at the individual level. For example, the bureaucratic structure of government has no counterpart on an individual level. The same is true for the market place. At this point, we noted that, in contrast to the description of institutions, actions taken by society and actions taken by individuals (while perhaps differing in specific content), could be classified under categories which were equally valid at the societal and at the personal level. For instance, the disagreements arising between two government agencies such as the Department of Health, Education and Welfare and the Department of Labor could be classified as *Conflict*. The disagreements which occur between two individuals could also be classified as *Conflict*. It was found that certain other concepts denoting action, such as *Power* and *Valuing*, were equally applicable to both levels. The effort, then, was to achieve a range of *action-concepts* which could refer to all the known aspects of citizenship education at the societal and personal levels.

It was further felt that *action-concepts*, ahistorical in nature, i.e., not typical of a specific time or place, could more fully provide a logically powerful curriculum design. Since history could be a source of specific topics, there was no urgency to deal with the historical in the design. The *action-concepts* so conceived promised a broadly based open curriculum structure.

THE SOCIAL STUDIES CURRICULUM CENTER AT SYRACUSE UNIVERSITY PAVES THE WAY

From 1963 to 1968, the Social Studies Curriculum Center at Syracuse University engaged in an effort to revise the social studies curriculum of both the elementary and secondary schools. Among its major contributions was its effort to identify the most important concepts from the social sciences and allied disciplines appropriate for elementary and secondary social studies programs.[2] Since the Syracuse Center had made a serious effort to achieve a list of concepts which were open-ended, broad in scope, and sufficiently unique to warrant inclusion in a social studies curriculum—all criteria which were compatible with those recognized by us—it was felt that the Syracuse effort would be a valid starting point to begin the search for *action-concepts*.

The Syracuse list was first reviewed in its entirety. Each of the 34 concepts was then independently considered. The Center had disavowed any attempt to reach "a comprehensive conceptual structure for the social studies curriculum."[3] The reason given was that the disciplines had "no reasonably agreed upon structure to offer."[4] The contributors of the Center appear to have assumed that the only source for structured curriculum design was the disciplines. This was in contrast with our recognition of the many sources of curriculum content outside the disciplines.

Nevertheless, in constructing their list, the disciplines were abandoned in favor of such interdisciplinary topics as "The Industrialization-Urbanization Syndrome,"[5] "Secularization,"[6] "Power,"[7] "Scarcity,"[8] "The Modified Mar-

[2]Roy A. Price, Gerald R. Smith, and Warren L. Hickman, *Major Concepts for Social Studies*, Syracuse University: The Social Studies Curriculum Center, November 1965.
[3]*Ibid.*, p. 7.
[4]*Op. cit.*
[5]*Ibid.*, p. 9.
[6]*Ibid.*, p. 10.
[7]*Ibid.*, p. 11.
[8]*Ibid.*, p. 12.

ket Economy,"[9] the "Dignity of Man,"[10] "Empathy,"[11] and so forth. The Center had clearly stressed the interactive qualities of the different elements which comprise society and had, indeed, escaped the restrictions of the disciplines. The abandonment of the disciplines in favor of broad topics is actually recognition of the fundamental distinction between the social sciences and the social studies.

The Syracuse list of concepts for the social studies flounders on at least two counts. The most obvious is its lack of logical ordering. For example, "Power" is placed in the same dimension as "The Industrialization-Urbanization Syndrome" with no apparent rationale. Urbanization is an historic phenomena arising out of the particular conditions of a particular time. It is a result of a long line of causations. Power exists ahistorically. Its exercise is apparent as long as there is life and even without life, in the operations of nature. It is an activity that achieves results. It is not excluded from the process of urbanization, but is necessary if urbanization is to occur. Urbanization is in no way necessary to power.

The second problem arises with the realization that many of the concepts suggested are only indirectly concerned with the citizen or the models he uses in significant decision making. Manifested in the list is a stress on how the society is functioning. In fairness, it should be noted that under the concept, "Morality and Choice," it is recognized that the citizen ". . . must deliberate upon decisions and participate in both making and effecting these decisions."[12] Nevertheless, the Syracuse concepts, with few exceptions, are based on the society and what the citizen should understand about his society. While not

[9]*Ibid.*, p. 14.
[10]*Ibid.*, p. 23.
[11]*Ibid.*
[12]*Ibid.*, p. 12.

wishing to underestimate the importance of comprehending the ongoing functions of one's society, it occurs to us
that it is equally important for the citizen to understand
how he, the citizen, goes about reaching conclusions,
making decisions, and acting upon decisions. He should
learn to examine his position as well as his society's
position. It is not enough to say that social change can
occur when most of what is studied deals with existing
conditions. From this stress on the actual state of society,
it is a short leap to the assumption that what is, is all that
is possible. Even "change" can be drawn into the conception of what is possible so that only certain types of
change are thought about.

The explanations accompanying the Syracuse concepts
are jaded with phrases that reveal the tendency to accent,
above all, what is, rather than exploring what could be.
Some examples follow:

> Most important the child should learn that for all the
> varieties of conflict there are culturally approved and
> disapproved means for resolving them.[13]

> As the heart of one of the most serious problems fac-
> ing the world today, this concept should be a part of
> every student's preparation for citizenship in the
> world of tomorrow.[14]

> If a citizen hopes to comprehend political science he
> must appreciate that in political science the element
> of power is concerned with those power-relationships
> which have consequences through instrumentalities of
> government.[15]

The list of phrases reiterating the citizen's need to understand *what is* could be considerably extended. At the

[13]*Ibid.*, p. 9.
[14]*Ibid.*, p. 10.
[15]*Ibid.*, p. 12.

same time, perhaps unintentionally, the citizen's understanding of other societies as well as his own identity as
an individual have been pushed to the background. In
this way, the citizen's capability for social criticism and
invention is greatly reduced.

The trend taken by the Syracuse concepts may, in part,
be due to the emphasis placed on the social science disciplines (even though this emphasis is not borne out by
the suggested list). The social science disciplines do not
get involved with how the citizen goes about making his
decisions. Nor are they particularly interested in the
continual disharmonies and changes which occur in
everyday life and which seem to follow no discernible
law. The Syracuse concepts are geared to handle conclusions with regard to society in general as these are
reflected in the disciplines. There seems to be little room
for questions of personal relevance. The *action-concepts*,
under which individual and societal concerns can be dealt
with equally, appear to offer a remedy for this serious
lacking.

Each of the Syracuse concepts was considered from the
perspective of *action-concepts*. Among those eliminated
either because they were static in nature, or were not
applicable at both the societal and personal levels, or
were not sufficiently ahistorical, were the following.

> Sovereignty of the Nation-State in the Community
>   of Nations
> The Industrialization-Urbanization Syndrome
> Secularization
> The Modified Market Economy
> Habitat and Its Significance
> Institution
> Social Control
> Social Change
> Scarcity

Dignity of Man
Empathy
Loyalty
Government by Consent of the Governed
Freedom and Equality

This in no way means that these concepts are not excellent sources of content for the social studies, but simply that the areas covered by them do not sufficiently coincide with the criteria for a curriculum structure based on *action-concepts*.

The characteristics of inherent nobility and worth which accompany the "Dignity of Man" could not be attributed to establishments of the society. One may talk about the efficiency of the Pentagon but not of its inherent nobility and worth. The concept of a "market" must necessarily presuppose large numbers of buyers and sellers interacting with each other. It would make no sense to buy from or sell to oneself. "Loyalty," which was defined as the devotion to a greater cause than oneself, would only make sense on a societal level if the society actively accepted a greater cause than itself. God might be such a cause, but this kind of cause is historical in nature. There are many societies that do not accept anything greater than themselves. "Scarcity" brought to mind its companion on the scale, "Affluence" (we wonder why it had not been included). This thought brought with it the realization that we were dealing with an historical phenomenon. We, in America, are in an age of plenty; others are in a period of scarcity. History has even brought the same society through scarcity and plenty. Furthermore, both "Scarcity" and "Affluence" could be covered under such *action-concepts* as *Power* and *Valuing*.

It was with some reluctance that "Habitat and Its Significance" was excluded. As with some of the other categories, it was clearly a *nonaction-concept*. However, it was equally clear that its applicability was both personal and societal, that it could be (though not necessarily) ahistorical, and that it was a major determinant in the life of both the individual and the society. However, it was also realized that questions regarding the habitat could be included as topical input rather than as part of the overall curriculum design of the course. The content covered by habitat was in no way comparable to the extension of such *action-concepts* as *Power* and *Conflict*, each one of which could support not only a unit on habitat, but on any of the Syracuse concepts excluded above. For instance, while *Power* could be treated in the context of "Empathy" as affective power, and so forth, "Habitat" would be impossible to treat in the context of "Empathy" or in the context of the "Sovereignty of the Nation-State in the Community of Nations."

It was equally difficult to eliminate "Freedom and Equality." Freedom could most certainly operate as a category on the personal and societal levels. However, when analyzed, it was determined that freedom is a state of being having no meaning without the explication of such action-concepts as *Power*. When we are free to act, we immediately find *Conflict, Valuing, Power*, etc., in operation and our freedom is a description of the permissiveness accompanying *Power, Valuing, Conflict*, etc.

Eleven of the Syracuse concepts were presented as methodological approaches and techniques. Among these were:

Historical Method and Point of View
The Geographical Approach
Causation
Observation, Classification, and Measurement
Analysis and Synthesis
Questions and Answers

Objectivity
Skepticism
Interpretation
Evaluation
Evidence

The list is a mixture of intellectual tools, of disciplinary approaches, and of teaching aids. "Observation, Classification, and Measurement," "Analysis and Synthesis," "Objectivity," "Skepticism," "Interpretation," "Evaluation," and "Evidence," are easily placed among the intellectual tools desirable for the student to develop and improve. They are simply some of the ways used by the citizen to improve his models. The list might be extended to include other powerful intellectual tools such as retroduction and inversion. In short, these intellectual tools should be treated under the source for models which we, earlier in this work, chose to call "models of formal analysis." Taken alone, these intellectual tools are inadequate for the development of a social studies curriculum design. A curriculum structure based on them would give almost no guidance for content input. If there is any point to curriculum development, it is in the guidelines for content selection, which, in turn, underlines what is most important to think about. Thinking about a given area of content in no way means that the development of the student's intellectual tools will not be encouraged. Indeed, we have looked upon intellectual models as appropriate sources for topic development. Furthermore, these tools must be continually brought into play if any of the goals of citizenship education are to be attained.

Knowing how to pose "Questions and Answers" is one of the most vital instructional aids at the disposal of the teacher. "Evaluation" is similarly interpretable as both an intellectual tool and as a teaching aid used to communicate to the student how well he is learning or to assess how well the teacher is teaching. These two concepts were also considered as not belonging to the social studies content sources, but as tools to work with any content. They are not sufficient guides for content selection.

"Historical Method and Point of View" and "The Geographical Approach" clearly belong to two of the sources for decision-making models already described. It has been asserted that history and the social science disciplines are major sources from which the citizen may obtain his models. The two concepts presented by the Syracuse group are action oriented insofar as they are inquiry models associated with history and geography. But every discipline, to be a discipline, offers models for ways of thinking. These are highly particularized models. It is what Bruner has called the "psychology of a subject."[16] While "Historical Method and Point of View" and "The Geographical Approach" to represent dynamic approaches to model development, their scope is clearly limited to the disciplines that have fostered them. Thus, the type of content dealt with would be limited. Certainly, their validity as topical input is unquestionable, but as a basis for developing a social studies design they are too narrow. We wonder why the Syracuse study omitted consideration of inquiry models provided by the other social science disciplines. In any case, discipline-based inquiry models do not meet the criterion for personal relevance posited in this work.

"Causation" was the object of considerable debate. The concept of cause and effect is a vital understanding in the intellectual development of the student. However, rather than being narrow in scope, "Causation" could include all conceivable actions occurring in this world.

[16]Jerome S. Bruner, *Toward a Theory of Instruction*, Cambridge: The Belknap Press, 1966, p. 154.

In other words, to be manageable as part of an educational design, categories for "Causation" would have to be determined. It seems to us that the *action-concepts* represent an effort to do precisely this. Our ways of valuing are causes for given effects. The uses of power each have a range of effects. Thus, although the concept "Causation" has been eliminated, it is indirectly present in the *action-concepts* which we propose to use.

Another concept—"Culture"—not included among methodological approaches of the Syracuse list exhibits a similar characteristic of all-inclusiveness which would necessarily have to be subdivided into manageable categories. It occurred to us that here too the *action-concepts* could serve as categories of culture. The way conflicts are resolved are manifestations both of a society's culture, and of the way an individual exercises his culture.

The remaining concepts of the Syracuse list were considered as candidates for the development of *action-concepts*. These were:

> Conflict—Its Origin, Expression, and Resolution
> Compromise and Adjustment
> Comparative Advantage
> Power
> Morality and Choice
> Input and Output
> Saving
> Interaction

In reviewing these concepts, it was felt that a more tightly constructed list could be achieved by making each of the categories comparable in both extension and nature. "Conflict," which had been presented as necessarily following a regular pattern inevitably ending with resolution, was freed from these limitations so that it could be on the same level of generalization and of personal and societal applicability as *Power*. "Input and Output," which the Syracuse list restricted to the industrial context, was considered to be a characteristic of *Power* in a mass-production society and was eliminated in favor of this action-concept. "Saving," which is an accumulation of possessions, is another facet of the Syracuse concept of "Power." The security which is achieved through saving is a result of the increased power felt by the saver. Therefore, "Saving" was also subsumed under the *action-concept, Power*. The conception of "Interaction" was broadened so that it included not only the regular relationships between individuals, but the regular relationships between institutions, and between institutions and individuals. In this sense, *Interaction* is the *action-concept* of the traditional ways institutions and people operate. The extension and nature of *Interaction* were thus brought more closely into line with *Power* and *Conflict*. "Morality and Choice" was relabeled *Valuing*, which underlines more clearly the influence upon action that ethics holds—indeed the "oneness" that ethics and action frequently have between them. "Compromise and Adjustment" and "Comparative Advantage" seemed to closely overlap so that it was determined to group them under one *action-concept, Adjustment*, which could refer to any type of adjustment including compromise and selection based on comparative advantage. *Adjustment* was also seen as operating on the personal as well as the societal levels and as covering a sufficiently broad area of content from which decision-making models are derived.

At this point, having worked with all the concepts presented by the Syracuse Center, it was realized that a vital area of action still had not been dealt with. This was *Change*. In eliminating "social change" because it was clearly intended as a societal characteristic, the idea of change itself had been lost, for the Syracuse group had not treated it except as a societal concept. We felt that

Change was a vitally important *action-concept* which was equally applicable at the societal and personal levels.

In all, six major *action-concepts* were identified. They are as follows:

> Conflict
> Power
> Valuing
> Interaction
> Change
> Adjustment

The six *action-concepts* would seem to include all conceivable forms of human action on both the personal and the societal level. They offer the school a logical pedagogical structure for dealing with human behavior. The number of topics that could be chosen for study under these concepts approaches infinity. Thus, *flexibility* and *structure* are achieved at one and the same time.

6 The Structure of Social Education Based on the Action-Concepts

AN ELABORATION OF THE ACTION-CONCEPTS

Before the *action-concepts* can become adequate elements of a curriculum design, the ranges of content to which they refer must be clarified. Such clarification is necessary in order to ascertain that a maximum completeness of study has been accomplished for each *action-concept*. It is also necessary so that the materials developed will deal with a manageable area of learning, will cover the full range of sources, and will be consistent and relatable to each other in a way that will contribute to the logical whole.

The effort has been made to define each *action-concept* and to map its structure for pedagogical use. Our goal in defining and explicating the six *action-concepts* is to suggest their relationship to specific topics. The definitions, and their accompanying structures and examples, follow.

CONFLICT: An Incompatability Among Societal and/or Personal Elements Which Interferes with the Functioning of Those Elements

There may be a number of elements undergoing conflict in a society and the society will still be able to function adequately. This is also true at the personal level. There is a point, however, beyond which the proliferation of conflicts will mean the disintegration of the society, or of the individual.

Conflict may exist at a number of levels vital to the citizen and to the decisions he must make. The goals, roles, and instruments of life appear to be the major areas of conflict development. Contradictory goals may be found on a scale ranging from the intimate or personal to the completely societal. Goal conflicts frequently exist among the personal goals of the individual (intraindividual). For instance, the individual may desire to lead a well-balanced family life with a good deal of time spent in shared family activities. On the other hand, he may also desire to "get ahead," to be a financial success, and he may find himself working harder and harder while having less and less time to devote to his family life. Conflicting goals frequently arise not only within the individual, but between individuals (interindividual). Two individuals may want the same job. Their conflict may be characterized by friendly competition or by open hostility.

There are numerous conflicts between the goals held by individuals and goals held by societal institutions. These individual-institutional goal conflicts begin to arise almost as soon as the individual has contact with a public institution. The child may have no interest or inclination to learn arithmetic while the school will insist that he do so. The child may be interested in collecting pictures of baseball stars while the school requires him to know the names of political leaders. Outside of the school, the child continues to encounter individual-institutional conflicts. He wants a new game; the company that produces the game wants money and will not let him have the game unless he pays—which he frequently cannot do. In adulthood, such individual-institutional goal conflicts continue. The blue-collar worker may want a sense of personal achievement, while the company, interested in efficiency, may persist in dividing the work so that the worker may never have a feeling of true accomplishment. He may go on producing the same little piece for years without ever coming in contact with the finished product. The goal to be an independent thinker also comes in conflict with the goals of industry to prepare the purchasing market so well that the sale of a mass-produced item will be virtually assured even before the item is out on the market. If the buyer has been prepared so that he will inevitably buy, he is obviously not exercising much independent thinking.

Goal conflicts may also exist within an institution (intrainstitutional). Governmental departments are particularly prone to this type of conflict. The Department of Health, Education and Welfare may truly desire the maximum improvement in the health, education, and welfare of this nation's citizens. It also desires the continuation of its existence. This continuation frequently depends on political considerations. Thus, it may abandon effective programs for improving health, education, and welfare for political purposes. There may be a request for less funds than are necessary for a project to continue successfully because the political party in power has begun a general economy drive. A highly qualified individual may be eliminated because of his political leanings. The department's goal of political survival conflicts with the department's goal to benefit the public's health, education, or welfare.

There are also goal conflicts between different institutions (interinstitutional). Interinstitutional goal conflicts can be found between universities and industry. College requisites for the high school graduate differ radically from the requisites which industry hold for the high school graduate. The same scholastic institutions are expected to handle these exceedingly different sets of requisites frequently with exactly the same equipment. There are other examples. Movie production companies have achieved considerable financial success with the so-called "adult films." Their goal is primarily a high box-office attendance. Censorship groups, organized primarily to preserve existing morals, will often conflict violently with film makers. The city and state governments often hold goals which are at odds. The state government may aim to primarily please its rural population while the city government may aim to satisfy the needs of its urban population. Thus, there are continual conflicts over what taxes shall be levied and how revenues shall be distributed.

Conflict exists at every level of organization devised by man. Both intrasocietal and intersocietal conflicts are increasing in frequency and magnitude as questions of communication and transportation become technologically insignificant. Of course, there is not always a clear line of demarcation between interinstitutional conflicts and intrasocietal conflicts. The President and Congress have already clashed over what the real powers of the President as Commander-in-Chief of the Armed Forces are regarding the Vietnam War. At the same time, the long harangue concerning the morality of United States participation in the Vietnam War is a clear example of intrasocietal conflict. There are many who societally value the fact that the United States has never lost a war. There are others who believe that whether the United States wins or loses is unimportant. What matters is that they interpret American action as imperialistic and, therefore, morally wrong. They do not believe that the Vietnamese pose a direct threat to this nation. The conflict between those who would not have us be an imperialistic society and those who believe in the greatness of our nation under any and all circumstances is an open and violent one. Furthermore, the opposition of other nations to United States policy in Vietnam constitutes an example of intersocietal conflict. The role envisioned by the United Nations is basically one of bringing peaceful settlement to intersocietal conflicts.

Role conflicts are frequently (though not necessarily) directly related to goal conflicts. The accent shifts from goals to the characteristics of people holding the goals. As individuals carry conflicting goals with them, so too do they bear roles which are logically incompatible (intraindividual). For example, a man may be both a father and a policeman. The man's son is found in some illegal activity. As a father he feels obliged to protect his son. As a policeman he feels obliged to arrest him. A child may be both a good student and a friendly fellow liked by his peers. As he grows older it becomes more and more difficult to live up to the characteristics of a good student and still be a fellow generally liked by his peers. If he studies long hours he may be snickered at and called a square. If he does not join in a classroom ruckus, he may be thought a sissy or, worse, teacher's spy. Even being an ordinary citizen is a role that conflicts with the role of the voter. Because the ordinary citizen is "ordinary," he is deprived of information with regard to war, foreign diplomacy, new inventions, and so forth. Because the voter votes with regard to these and other problem areas, he should have the information which he is deprived of as an ordinary citizen.

Role conflicts exist between individuals as well (inter-individual). In the school, the teacher may see himself as fundamentally an objective, normathetic individual who is simply trying to impart the culture of his society (which is what he is being paid for). The student may consider himself a prisoner obliged to stay in school; his warden is his teacher. In the same way, the role of a civil servant may conflict with the role of an elected politician. The civil servant may see his job as a respectable though hum-drum way of earning a living. He is not being paid much—why should he overwork? The elected politician may see himself as a reformer of civil service institutions. Civil servants are not doing what they are paid to do and so it is time to crack down.

The last area of conflict development that we have dealt with is perhaps the most difficult to explain. Instrumental conflict is somewhat detached from goal conflicts and role conflicts insofar as the emphasis is upon the means used for obtaining a goal or fulfilling a role. These means have by-products which may interfere with the attainment of the goals or prevent the fulfillment of desired roles. For example, a system of testing and grading may be used in the schools as an incentive to encourage the child to study the content he needs to know. The instrument conflicts with its own purposes for one of its by-products is to encourage the child to study only when a grade will be given and not for the sake of knowing the content. A similar instrumental conflict occurs when, in order to teach how democracy works, the schools adopt a replicative form of democratic voting procedures, asking children to vote for a class president. Since there are no real issues and no real knowledge regarding the qualification of candidates, the election becomes a popularity contest. Children are taught to vote on the basis of whether they like the way the candidate smiles or talks rather than on what he stands for. In adult life, instances of instrumental conflict continue to multiply. The media are means of diffusing information but frequently there is no distinction with regard to the importance of the information. Thus a local accident may be newscast more often than reports on the progress of a disarmament conference. The citizen is so bombarded with useless information that he may simply tune out.

The structure of the *action-concept, Conflict,* to be used as a guide for topical input, is given below in outline form.

CONFLICT

I. Goal Conflicts
   A. Individual
      1. Intraindividual
      2. Interindividual
   B. Individual-institutional
   C. Institutional
      1. Intrainstitutional
      2. Interinstitutional
   D. Societal
      1. Intrasocietal
      2. Intersocietal
II. Role Conflicts
   A. Intraindividual
   B. Interindividual
III. Instrumental Conflicts

POWER: The Exercise of Means in a Manner Such That a Societal Element or Group of Elements Can Control Another Societal Element or Group of Elements in at Least One Aspect

The definition of power that has been presented here is limited to the human context. Power may be exercised outside of human society. Gases have the power of heat emanating from them. Light is a form of power that may emanate from the stars or the sun. They do not use their power with the intention of controlling other elements of existence such as the darkness or the cold. The intentional use of power in logically consistent fashions so as to achieve increasing control over a growing number of elements is the uniquely human characteristic of power.

Power exercised within the societal framework has various origins. The characteristics of those origins leave their imprint on the power being exercised. Thus, power based on force exhibits characteristics which are quite different from power based on love. Power may be biological in origin, i.e., the ability to control depends on the innate qualities of individuals. Physical qualities such as size, strength, and speed may be increased with practice; but they cannot be acquired, they must be born with the individual. The same is true for many mental qualities. The ability to manipulate symbols, which enables the young child to gain command of a complex language, is innate. Mathematical ability, memory, and imagination are also abilities of mental power. Similarly, the human being is born with emotional capacity. Cultures will reinforce certain emotional qualities which predispose individuals and groups of individuals to behave in certain ways. Exactly how emotional power is achieved is unknown but that it exists is undeniable. Hitler, for instance, held great attraction for the Germans of the 1930s, which has often been recognized but never fully explained logically.

Power may also depend on the possessions of elements which are needed, or desired in a given society. For example, the possession of certain animate and inanimate tools so increases man's innate biological powers that these tools are highly desirable. The wheel increased man's ability to move heavy objects as well as his speed.

The harnessing of the horse increased these powers; the car, with its addition of the motor, has extended physical, biological powers even further. In the same way, possessions have also increased man's mental powers. Possession of the computer has increased the span of human memory toward what may well be infinity. Mathematical ability has been similarly extended.

The possession of money or some such forms of wealth yields power which is not an extension of the biological. Money is a product of human agreement within a given society. That is, members agree (whatever the reasons) that gold or silver or wampum or dollars are of such significance that they can be used to acquire other possessions. Both people and institutions are willing to strive for money for it may then be transformed, through buying or trading, into the desired objects. Thus, those who possess a form of money possess considerable control over the actions of people and institutions. For example, a small town has a large industry located within its limits. The taxes received from the company permit better schools or improved streets. There may also be considerable pollution emanating from the company's smoke stacks. There may even be a law against such pollution but the townsmen hesitate to enforce such a law because the company has threatened to move away and stop paying the taxes which have so enriched the treasury. On an individual level, money increases a child's possibility of having more experiences, such as traveling or having a large number of books in his home, which have in turn a positive effect on the child's intellectual development.

Money is a fluid form of wealth which is largely symbolic in nature. There are more tangible and endurable forms of wealth such as land, buildings, and stores. The possible uses of these are what make them valuable. Land may be planted, buildings may be lived in, and stores may be used to display one's wares. The value of their uses is often the gauge of the wealth they represent. An owner may possess a store in a strategic location. He may operate the store himself and be in a better position to obtain business than other store owners. He may also choose to rent his store. His profit may even be as high as that of the individual who is operating the business, and he, the owner, is not working in it at all.

Power is also derived from expertise. In this case, control depends on the knowledge of certain skills needed or desired by others. Such control may be held by individuals, or it may reside in institutions. The possession of a car alone does not insure that the owner will be capable of using the car. The knowledge concerning the proper operations of a car is the expertise of the driver, and the owner may have to give of his wealth in order to have an expert drive his car. A medical doctor offers expertise with regard to health so that our biological powers may be better preserved. A lawyer offers expertise and protection of the law which we, on our own, would be unable to attain. A stockbrokerage firm offers institutional expertise upon which the individual purchaser of stock is dependent. The church offers theological expertise for which the ordinary layman feels the need. If we have money or some form of wealth we will probably be in a position to avail ourselves of these experts. If we have nothing valuable to give in exchange, we may give up the benefit of certain experts.

The exercise of authority is another form of power. The origin of control lies in the acceptance of certain ways of interacting, guiding individuals and institutions. There is inherited authority typified by a king who inherits his role of dominating others regardless of his own expertise, wealth, or biological abilities. In a democratic society, the voter inherits his powers in much the same way. There is also authority vested in individuals and groups by way of tradition. In many societies, there is the obligation to obey one's mother and father long after the need to obey is gone. Furthermore, institutions with or without tradition, may vest authority in certain individuals. The teacher, the policeman, the President of the United States are examples of people who carry institutional authority. Whole institutions may also be powerful by means of the authority vested in them. The FBI and the CIA are powerful institutions not simply for the possessions and expertise at their command, but because they are recognized as authorities. A biology teacher, because he is a teacher, will be closely listened to in a classroom situation. A student who may be as expert as the teacher and who tries to talk about his knowledge to fellow students in the classroom would either be ignored or thought overbearing. He lacks the power of institutional authority.

Religions become sources of power precisely because people believe in them and assign to them attributes which are not fully understood nor possessed by any human being. So long as belief continues in the religion, control over those who believe will continue. Representatives of religious power often wield considerable worldly influence. Because religious power is not clearly understood, the individuals who interpret the religion come to be accepted as exercising the powers attributed to the religion.

Religious power may operate at several levels of belief. Superstitions are unsystematic, unproved beliefs regarding the way things happen in life. Frequently, considerable power is attributed to superstitions. A penny found on some street or other is supposed to bring good fortune to one's life. A four-leaf clover is also supposed to bring luck. The ace of spades in a deck of cards is an evil omen that may signify death. The stars are claimed to exert power on our human lives. The list goes on and on.

These heterogeneous beliefs may be unified under the concept of superstition primarily because they are unsystematic and unproved. There are no consistent assumptions save that some nonliving objects in the world hold an unexplainable influence over human life. Why some objects and not others is never clear.

Mythological beliefs differ from superstition in several ways. They are, for one, more systematically developed. They primarily deal with supernatural conceptions of humanity. These supernatural conceptions take two forms: human beings are viewed with extraordinary qualities and are thus gods or demi-gods; and human beings who are no longer living in this world live on in some other world and may be contacted. The classic gods of the Greeks and the relationships between these gods and the people, bringing them good or ill-fortune, is an example of mythological beliefs. Also examples of mythological beliefs are the seances, which are still popular today and which attempt to reach the dead. In both cases, there is claimed to be interaction between the natural and the supernatural. An explanation for existence that would encompass humanity in a total conception of life, death, time, space, the universe, and so forth may be present, but it is not necessary to mythological beliefs which place emphasis on earthly life.

Religions make the effort to find a total explanation for human existance. While usually retaining some emphasis on human-superhuman contact in daily life, the major effort is to justify what is done in this life within a much broader context, and usually in the light of some sort of after-life. Origins of life are, however, vital concerns and frequently lay the basis for those assumptions upon which a highly structured system of beliefs is built.

Religious manifestations vary widely from culture to culture—even the same religion may take different forms within different cultures. Thus African dances have been incorporated in the Catholic rites performed in Africa, while any form of dancing is almost unknown in the Catholic rites of North America. These "earthly" practices, guided by religious leaders, are usually the means through which religious leaders acquire "earthly" power. For example, in Catholicism one has the responsibility of going to church. If one does not attend a service on Sunday, one should seek a pardon from the priest. Of course, the priest can only give a pardon in God's name. The strength in the religious belief will be reflected in the power which the priest will be able to wield on earth because it is he and he alone who can grant God's pardon.

Power is also derived from the banding together of individuals into formal and informal groups. "Groupness" itself serves as a base of power. The very fact that a group exists creates power. The quantity of control achieved by groups may depend on such factors as size, expertise, cohesiveness, possessions, purpose, etc. Groups may vary from the informal, with shifting or unestablished goals, to the formal or institutional, with clearly understood objectives and established means. Groups of long standing may continue to exercise power, however, even after the original goals have lost their validity. Groups exert control not only externally on other groups and individuals, but on their membership. An individual member may himself be in conflict with some of the objectives of his group, but his acting will nevertheless be in conformity with the group.

"Groupness" is a source of power which may be in part psychological in origin, resting on the need of the individual to belong. However, exactly how power is derived from "groupness" has not been logically understood as yet. Furthermore, "groupness" is always accompanied by the exercise of other forms of power, i.e., possessions, authority, and so forth. This makes it very difficult to isolate "groupness" in a power configuration.

Nevertheless, the validity of its existence must be recognized here.

Power derived from "groupness" may be studied as groups relate to individuals or as groups relate to each other. The society, which is the sum of groups and individuals exercising power, may also be seen as deriving power from its "groupness." In this sense, society is a compromise of the powers exercised by its various elements. While individuals and groups can still exercise control upon the society, the society, from the strength of this compromise of powers, is also capable of exercising control over individuals and groups. Whether the uniqueness of societal power means that the society is a superorganic entity remains a highly debatable question which would certainly make interesting fare for the classroom study of *Power*.

Additionally, societal power must be viewed from two major perspectives—as a phenomenon of a particular society, and as a phenomenon of international relationships. Internationally, the types and degrees of powers available to societies or nations will vary widely. For instance, a society may possess considerably more economic and military power than other societies, yet will be unable to participate at international meetings as authoritatively as other weaker nations are able to do. A democratic form of government may force the representatives of a society to return to various components of the society for authorization. A dictatorship will not have such restrictions and will be able to act more authoritatively and probably more effectively diplomatically than a stronger, democratic society.

Societal power at the international level must be studied as though it were a stable entity of a superorganic nature. Each society reveals certain characteristics in the exercise of power which will place it in a particular position with regard to other societies. While internally these characteristics may be subject to change through the actions of internal societal components, if the international power play is to be grasped at all, a certain stability of characteristics must be assumed. It must be possible to say the French are powerful in this or that way even though there is considerable turmoil within France with regard to how the French wish to exercise power.

A superorganic treatment of society for the purposes of study does not mean that societies are superorganic. Thus, the school must guard against its own mechanisms for study so that conceptions are not assumed as truths but debated as possibilities.

The structure or extension of *Power* to be used as a guide for topical content input is given below in outline form.

POWER
  I. Biological
      A. Physical
      B. Mental
      C. Emotional
 II. Possession
      A. Wealth
          1. Money
          2. Property: Land, buildings, stores
      B. Animate and inanimate tools extending biological power
III. Expertise
      A. Individual
      B. Institutional
 IV. Authority
      A. Inherited
      B. Traditional
      C. Institutional
  V. Religious
      A. Superstition

     B. Mythology
     C. Religion
  VI. "Groupness"
     A. Informal
     B. Formal (including institutional)
     C. Societal
     D. Intersocietal

VALUING: The Act of Estimating the Importance of Elements and Actions in Relation to Human Life

"Importance" is not a fixed concept but varies in quality as the situation varies. In a religious context, it may signify "spiritual worthiness," while in a specific, material situation it may mean "usefulness." Thus, in a Christian situation, "goodness" is important and highly valued. In the situation of nailing a picture on a wall, a "hammer" is important and highly valued. However, "goodness" and "hammer" are not interchangeable. The context of each has made each important in a different way. Therefore, the act of valuing may be characterized by determining the type of contexts within which the concept of importance operates.

There is, for example, the individual-material situation in which the individual attributes importance to some material object. The material object may already exist in nature. It may also be a man-made product. The individual may attribute considerable value to the ownership of a car and be willing to pay a high price for one. A lovely countryside may be of no importance to the individual and so he continues to dump his litter anywhere that is convenient. The wood for furniture obtained from trees may be highly valued by the individual and he will cut down trees for that purpose. Trees for soil conservation may have little importance to the individual.

The individual-ethical situation occurs when the individual acts according to the criteria of "good" acting set either by the society, its institutions, or himself. There may be ample opportunity to cheat on a test with little risk of being caught. The individual might even need to cheat for a passing grade, but he decides not to do so. The societal criteria have influenced his acting. An automobile accident in which neither party is injured but for which one of the parties was completely to blame occurs. The other party could sue for much more than the worth of his car since he has undergone shock and considerable disturbance through no fault of his own. To sue would be an ethically acceptable act for the society. The innocent party, however, decides that it would be wrong to profit and perhaps put another individual into difficulty when he should be grateful just to be alive. He does not sue and by so doing acts according to an inner-directed ethical standard. Other individuals might consider this "personal" ethic silly.

The institutional-material situation occurs when large organized groups are involved in judging the importance of natural or societal objects. Maintaining a high level of production is greatly valued by most industries. Obsolescence may even be intentionally built into an industry's products so that consumer demands will warrant a continued high level of production. Lakes and rivers are particularly valued by steel companies not for the beauty of such waterways but for the convenience and lower production costs which these afford.

The institutional-ethical situation occurs with great frequency. For example, business is slow, but to lay off many workers could cause the entire community hardships. The ethical decision is whether to lay off as many workers as might be indicated by the particular industry's economic situation. A company may "lift" another company's invention, change it slightly so as to avoid legal complications, and market it. By industry standards this may be good business acumen and not "stealing." In any case, there is an ethical element involving institutional decision making.

Similarly, the society, as a whole, is continually involved in the act of valuing. As with the individual and the institution, societal valuing occurs in material and ethical contexts. That poverty should be eliminated from the American scene is a case of societal-material valuing. Equal educational opportunity for all is another example of societal-material valuing. Great importance is attributed to the equal qualifications of teachers, to the equality of available equipment, to the opportunity of encountering students from a range of racial and socio-economic backgrounds, and so forth. The societal-ethical context is obviously closely related to this last example. The avowed ideal is that there should be no prejudice against minority groups because of race, creed, or national origin. (However, individual-ethical valuing may also be operating. An individual may not be prejudiced toward the American Indian or the Negro, and yet be prejudiced toward a disagreeably clothed hippie. Acts of valuing frequently lead to conflict.) Other instances of societal-ethical valuing are that freedom of the press is a right which should be protected, and that there should be freedom to worship.

This discussion of valuing has, up to this point, been contained within separate contexts having a given nature and occurring at a specific time and place. Acts of valuing may also occur simultaneously in overlapping contexts. The grades given by a university professor may involve ethical decisions with regard to the individual and to the institution. That is, the professor may believe that the individual should be encouraged in his studies. On the other hand, the university makes decisions concerning doctoral studies based on grades. The professor may want to encourage the poor student; he may also not want to misrepresent the abilities of the poor student to the university or some eventual employer. The professor is involved in the act of valuing his values. There is frequently the need to assign priorities to types of valuing. In the example of the professor, we have overlapping ethical situations. Overlapping material and ethical situations occur as well. Such examples have already been touched upon. When industry opts for obsolescence it has not given up the ideal of producing to the best of its ability or of selling an "honest" product to its customers. It simply has made a choice among overlapping value situations.

The assignment of priorities may occur not only because of overlapping situations happening historically, i.e., in a given time and place, but also independently of a specific historical context. Human life may be given more importance than animal life independently of any situation. Protecting the freedom of citizens may be valued more highly than efficient government operation in any time and in any place. Priority valuing which occurs ahistorically lays the foundations for the acting of any social group. The United States Constitution was developed largely through priority valuing.

The structure or extension of *Valuing* to be used as a guide for topical content input is given below in outline form.

VALUING
I. Situational Valuing
   A. Individual-material
   B. Individual-ethical
   C. Institutional-material
   D. Institutional-ethical
   E. Societal-material
   F. Societal-ethical

II. Priority Valuing
   A. Overlapping contexts
   B. Ahistorical contexts, i.e., valuing which applies outside of a specific time or place

INTERACTION: The Stable State of Relationships Which Compose the Underlying Cohesion of Societal Institutions and Societal Members

The concept of "status quo" when applied to society must be clarified. A society in status quo is not one in which everything has ceased to operate so that a kind of perfect immobility is achieved. The movement of humanity is inevitably the movement of society. Men eat, work, love, and play not only as individuals but as members of their society. This constant human interaction is continually creating patterns of living which can never be duplicated again. In a static society, however, these different patterns of living are sufficiently similar to the traditional standards so that they can be easily absorbed by the society. In other words, no significant change in the traditional standards is necessary to accommodate the activities of men or institutions. Such activities may be considered "normal" according to the established societal standards.

The changing of environmental settings, which occurs as individuals move from one place to another—for instance, from home to school—may appear to be phenomena of change, especially for those who are passing from one setting to another. Such differences are really phenomena of societal interaction. Changing settings and consequently going from one type of established function to another type of established function is a way of carrying out patterns of living within the limits traditionally established by the society.

In a large society, the normal interactions between individuals tend to become quite complex, because any one individual will participate in numerous interactions. Individual interaction may occur because of stable role relationships as husband-wife, child-mother-father, or retailer-wholesaler-consumer, for example. Stable role relationships abide by societally acceptable ways of acting. Business competitors are expected to try and "outdo" each other. A husband is expected to support his wife. A mother is expected to love her child even if it is a babbling idiot, etc.

Individual interaction may also occur while established roles are in the process of being assumed for the first time. A man and a woman meet, fall in love, get married, and have children. It is a perfectly traditional way of acting in our society and though the couple involved will feel an upheaval in their lives, their actions are manifestations of the status quo.

Interactions between individuals and institutions are also quite frequent. The interaction between school and pupil is an example of the stable role relationship. The pupil attends school for approximately 12 years; he follows one of several study programs considered useful for adult life; he cannot leave school until he has reached a certain age, etc. The child may also be viewed as becoming a member of the institution—a pupil. If the process of assuming a role is related to an institution, it is considered an institutional-individual interaction. If the role assumed is concerned with another individual, we would have an example of individual interaction. The bank lending money to a person so that he may build a house or a steel company's relations with its employees are examples of normally accepted ways of acting occurring between institutions and individuals.

Institutions may interact with other institutions. While in our society the school and the church are not supposed to interact directly, the home will have regular contact with both the school and the church. The community government will frequently support the schools making this interaction very crucial. Supporting the schools may be a long-established tradition of the community government. Suppose, however, that the community has grown and a special agency such as a metropolitan school system has been set up by the community to provide more efficient schooling. This agency will be in the process of assuming its role, which lies clearly within preestablished societal standards. The agency may not yet fully understand the needs of its schools or what the community really expects from its schools. These are understandings which the agency will attempt to acquire as it assumes its role.

Societal interaction exists between societies at the international level. The friendly relations between the United States and Canada have continued unchanged for so long they may be considered traditional and are an example of societal interaction. International agreements regarding such varied subjects as the treatment of prisoners of war, the uses of the ocean, and so forth are further instances of societal interaction.

The structure or extension of *Interaction* to be used as a guide for topical content input is given below in outline form.

INTERACTION
I. Individual
  A. Expected actions according to established roles
  B. Expected actions due to the assuming of roles accepted by societal standards
II. Individual–Institutional
  A. Expected actions according to established roles
  B. Expected actions due to the assuming of roles accepted by societal standards

III. Institutional
   A. Expected actions according to established roles
   B. Expected actions due to the assuming of roles accepted by societal standards
IV. Societal

CHANGE: A Dynamic Transforming of Characteristics so That They May Be Considered New or Essentially Different

The concept of "dynamic" has been used here not simply to indicate mobility, an attribute to be found in every kind of society, but to indicate characteristics which do not fit the societal standards. There is an element of nonconformity in dynamic change which may result in the change being unacceptable to the society as well as unpredictable regarding eventual outcomes.

In determining the major types of changes affecting both individual and societal acting, the biological transformations which all men undergo gave considerable pause for thought. It was reasoned that since biological growth or maturation in the human being was independent of human influences, it could not be considered a factor of human action and therefore would not be logically included under any of the *action-concepts* presented here. However, the quality of human biological change has never been fully determined. The tendency has been to separate genetic change and cultural change even though it has long been recognized that the environment plays a role in biological change. In the present state of knowledge and research, societal influence has permeated every stratum of the human environment. To the extent that the environment is culturally determined, biological change must be considered a result of human acting. What we are dealing with are biocultural changes. These seem to exist at two levels: within the actual formation of genetic potential, and after the potential has been established.

The phenomenon of selection operates at both levels. Mutations, which once might have been selected out, under present social conditions, might be selected in. For instance, the ethical attitude of a society dedicated to love and peace could very well mean the less marriage-ability of war-like people and their subsequent genetic elimination. A culture which admires slender, somewhat frail men might genetically eliminate muscular, stocky men. However, assuming that the genetic potential had not been eliminated, the cultural influence upon biologi-cal factors still operates. Potentially muscular, stocky men become less so because of the way they choose to treat their bodies. The small child, who could learn sev-eral native tongues but only learns one, has the remainder of his linguistic ability become a vestige somewhat like the appendix is believed to be. In other words, a range of genetic potential does not mean that societies will de-velop the potential fully or in the same ways. When certain potentials are ignored they become irretrievably lost as the human being matures.

It is frequently impossible to determine whether a physical change has taken place within the genes or after the genetic potential has been determined. For instance, the changing rate of sexual maturation which has accom-panied the accelerated pace of American living may be a change within the genes, or it may be a result of cultural influence on the existing genetic potential. What is rea-sonably certain is the cultural influence on such changes. The tendency of both sexes to look more and more alike, is, at least in part, a result of the diminishing difference in the cultural attitudes toward men and women.

Cultural change frequently occurs without subsequent biological modifications. These changes may come about as a result of changed sociological and psychological perceptions regarding status, self, institutions, goals, etc. Changed perceptions arise with new knowledge and/or new circumstances and/or new beliefs. The satus attributed to a hunter today is fundamentally different from the status he might have received during the early days of settlement on the North American Continent. New circumstances have reduced the importance of the hunter in our perception, changing his role as well. On the other hand, the astronaut today has steadily risen in importance. He is perceived as the "hunter" of the universe and excites our imagination. The view of American institutions is in a state of upheaval. The perception of American education has undergone a basic transformation. It is no longer the mecca of the poor through which they could hope to become true Americans and successful businessmen. Indeed, to many, education seems to mean "compulsory misguidance" perpetrated by a government intent on the status quo. To serve in the American army is becoming less and less a glorious deed to be applauded by all. Tax bureaus are frequently labeled dishonest monsters who expect honesty from the taxed, but not from themselves. Man's perceptions of man have undergone radical changes through the ages. From the individual intent on an after-life to an individual sure of his ability to acquire knowledge and control of the world, we seem now to be passing into a stage of pessimism toward the feats of humanity. The image is one of man, the puny midget of the universe, fooling himself into believing that he can control the immensity—or, even, that he counts in the immensity!

The most apparent type of change in our present world has been technological and scientific. Inventions, discoveries, and new scientific understandings have created not only new knowledge and new circumstances but new beliefs which have, in their turn, profoundly modified psychological-sociological perceptions. For instance, once having made a technological breakthrough, even if by accident, we have gone on systematically searching for improved ways of doing things. Having greatly increased our capacity to produce food, we now perceive the eventual elimination of poverty. Having invented the airplane we go on seeking inventions that will improve it or surpass it.

Technological discoveries as opposed to inventions are primarily based on an increasing knowledge of the elements man finds in nature and the environment surrounding him which, in turn, opens new fields of inventions. The discovery of fire made it possible to invent a host of machines including the steam engine. Man is continuing to develop medicines on the basis of herbs, molds, and the like which he finds operating in nature. At present, he is involved in discovering ways to harness atomic power. An invention may be necessary once he has discovered the underlying principles. Frequently, however, it will be a question of learning how to operate what is already in nature. Thus, gravity may be used to help man move heavy weights. A boat operates on the principle of displacement which occurs over and over in nature and which man simply has to discern in order to use for his own ends.

New scientific understandings have also contributed to profound changes in our world and to the ways that we perceive. The Ptolemeic theory of the universe was slow in succumbing to the Copernicus theory not for lack of empirical evidence, but primarily because religious conceptions would not permit acceptance of this new interpretation. When it was finally accepted, it meant an upheaval in man's way of thinking about himself in the world. Only a few decades ago, it was believed that the elements which comprise matter on this earth were immutable. The ancient alchemists who attempted to obtain gold by transforming other elements were considered superstitious screwballs. With the development of the atomic age, the transformation of elements into other elements appears entirely feasible. The idea is no longer perceived as being ridiculous. Science has acquired new empirical data which has led to new understandings concerning the composition of our environment.

Changing perceptions, sometimes based on technological developments, may lead to the desire for new institutions. New institutions may be invented from scratch, or existing institutions may be so modified that their goals and ways of functioning are essentially different. The Peace Corps is an example of a new institution based on changed perceptions of the international role of the United States and of the role of the young. The once highly autonomous corporation, though still maintaining the corporate form, has become increasingly a public institution for which profit making is a secondary goal. For example, Lockheed or the Penn Central Railroad continue operating with deficits and are subsidized by the government in order to achieve a desired public purpose.

Changes do not usually occur alone. There are a number of changes occurring simultaneously or in series, which influence each other as well as the societal status quo. Those changes which occur as a result of another change or group of changes may be classified in the category of "drift." Changes belonging to the phenomenon of drift are not intentional. They are frequently unintentional happenings. The improved means of transportation have led to an incredible increase in tourism and in the number of people who can travel for pleasure. Highly perfected tools of both an agricultural and industrial nature have decreased the amount of working time required from individuals. This, in turn, has changed the quality of the individual's available time so that he is as much at leisure as at work. The proliferation of electric appliances has profoundly changed what a woman needs to do in the home, and it has consequently given her a new attitude toward her own role as a housewife and as a human being. Medical science has succeeded in helping more people reach old age. In turn, this has created a society which has a large number of older people and no specific role available for them.

Changes may also arise through contacts between peoples of different cultural backgrounds. Such contacts may be of sufficient influence as to bring about basic changes in the original cultures involved. These contacts may occur at the very local level, as in an urban neighborhood. Here, individuals of different ethnic origins live together in very close quarters. Even while preserving their own ethnic backgrounds, they are being influenced by the ethnic backgrounds of their friends, neighbors, and business associates. For instance, on a walk through New York City today one can see signs advertising kosher salami, Mexican tacos, and French crepes.

On a broader scale, examples of intercultural contacts which have left their marks abound. The imperialism of Western Europeans leading to the invasions of foreign lands brought profound cultural changes in these lands that ran the gamut from religion to dress and transportation. The Norman invasion of England in 1066 left its impression on both the invaded and the invaders. The industrial influence of America can be easily observed in the smog-ridden Japan of today.

The cultural contacts discussed up to now are direct in nature, depending on a people-to-people relationship. Indirect cultural contacts are frequently powerful change agents, too. The books, movies, fads, styles, etc., which now travel so quickly from one country to another bear considerable influence. Let us remember that the long-haired boys of today first raised their heads in England.

The strikes of college campuses, which are so new to America, have been occurring at European universities for decades. Jazz, on the other hand, may be considered an American product which has borne its influence to a vast portion of the world.

The structure or extension of *Change* to be used as a guide for topical content input is given below in outline form.

CHANGE
  I. Biocultural
     A. Genetic potential
        1. Physical
        2. Mental
     B. Postgenetic potential
        1. Physical
        2. Mental
 II. Psychological-Sociological Perceptions
     A. Of self
     B. Of institutions
     C. Of status
     D. Of society
III. Technological-Scientific
     A. Invention
     B. Discovery
     C. Scientific understandings
 IV. Institutional
  V. Drift
 VI. Intercultural
     A. Direct
        1. Local: neighborhood, commune, region, etc.
        2. Intergroup
     B. Indirect
        1. International exemplars
        2. Individual travel

ADJUSTMENT: The Individual and Societal Efforts to Reach the Best Possible Equilibrium Among the Influences upon Human Life in Order to Achieve a Stability That Will Serve as a Reliable and Reasonably Predictable Basis for Human Activities

The conception of "equilibrium" has been limited to a societal context. The achievement of equilibrium occurs continually among natural phenomena. No matter where one looks in nature, there are systems which create an equilibrium of natural phenomena. The achievement of equilibrium is a question of the balance between different types of energy and different types of matter. If a given animal cannot fit into the balance, it is spontaneously eliminated by this very inability. The question of adjustment within the societal context is not dependent on such an extreme solution. Societal adjustment is never as complete as natural adjustment. Societal adjustment is dependent on at least three factors: the need to adjust, the capacity to adjust, and the will to adjust. Any one or all three of these factors may be operating as societal adjustment occurs.

While *Interaction* is descriptive of the functioning of society under established standards, and *Change* is reflective of the upheaval of such standards, *Adjustment* is the reassessment of societal functioning in order to regain equilibrium. Adjustments may occur in different realms of human activity. There are those activities which involve the individual and his material surroundings. (These include both natural and man-made materials.) The individual contributes heavily to air pollution through his considerable use of fuel-powered machines, thereby undermining his ability to breathe. Realizing the need to lessen air pollution does not mean that the individual will automatically give up the comforts he has acquired. It is more than probable that he will seek a compromise in his activities by looking for some means of controlling pollution that will permit the continued use of fuel-powered machines. If this effort is not successful soon enough, then a change in the use of these machines will be needed. If intentional adjustment or change within the societal context does not occur, the situation may go beyond man's control and natural adjustment will occur with the elimination of man, the major source of pollutant production.

Adjustments may occur within the individual (intraindividual) or among individuals (interindividual). For example, the individual may set high goals for himself in some undertaking but find that he is lacking in the necessary talents. To achieve equilibrium, he will have to adjust his expectations to reflect reality more closely.

Among individuals, adjustments may arise as a result of conflict. Some conflict situations among individuals lead to the use of power, and a subsequent adjustment dependent on the will of the victor and the capacity of the conquered to carry out that will. A teacher and his student may be in conflict about a particular assignment. The student may resist the assignment but capitulate to the professor's authority. Even so, the student may not have the ability to complete the assignment as conceived by the professor.

Many conflict situations among individuals are resolved without the use of power. There is, for instance, the realization that the interests of all concerned may best be achieved through compromise. Two landowners may be in conflict about the possession of a few acres of land. A legal battle would cost both owners dearly in time and money, and so they reach an agreement outside the courts.

Conflict need not be an active element in establishing

the need or desire for adjustment. Several scientists find they have been researching the same subject. They decide to pool their information and to continue their studies as a group. They perceive their advantage in working together but there is no real conflict. In a group situation, there may be several persons who have very valid contributions to make, but who also have dominant personalities which seem to make the other members of the group less willing to participate. Adjustment might be achieved by asking group members to first write out their ideas and then read their reports in turn.

Adjustments frequently occur between individuals and institutions. A school may set high admission standards but if an insufficient number of students meet those requirements, an adjustment in the standards will have to be made if the school is to continue as a school. Of course, adjustment does not always have to be acknowledged and open. That is, the school may continue to say that only the highest quality of student will be admitted while its interpretation of "high quality" may have been considerably modified. Congress passes tax laws which must be adjusted to the individual situation. Tax bureaus are really the agencies of such individual adjustments. Frequently, their policies change while the laws themselves have remained unchanged. This is a form of adjustment either toward individual needs and desires or toward government needs and desires.

There are intrainstitutional as well as interinstitutional adjustments. A public bureau such as the Department of State that is in the process of revising its bureaucratic systems is involved in a process of intrainstitutional adjustment most probably in the hopes of functioning more efficiently. Two museums of the same city and with essentially the same scope may avoid duplicating efforts by agreeing that each museum will specialize in some particular area. Their actions involve interinstitutional adjustment. For instance, one of the museums may have an art collection covering Western European history but specializing in Dutch and Spanish art, while the other museum may have a collection spanning the same historical period, but specializing in Italian art. Interinstitutional adjustment may also occur in what seem to be new forms. That is, a new institution is devised which will take over the activities of older institutions, thus eliminating these institutions, while substantially retaining the previously established goals. An example is the recent revision of postal service under an independent corporation.

Intrasocietal adjustments are frequent occurrences, especially regarding the ideals upheld by a whole society and the actual activities of that society. The society may be against imperialism while acting like an imperialistic nation. An adjustment of either the ideal or the action is likely to take place. Thus, *Imperialism* is adjusted to become foreign aid. Intersocietal adjustments involve world compromise. The manipulation of treaties and the like are examples of intersocietal adjustment. International adjustment is still in the first stages of development.

The structure or extension of *Adjustment* to be used as a guide for topical content input is given below in outline form.

ADJUSTMENT
  I. Individual-Material
 II. Individual
     A. Intraindividual
     B. Interindividual
III. Individual-Institutional
 IV. Institutional
     A. Intrainstitutional
     B. Interinstitutional
  V. Societal
     A. Intrasocietal
     B. Intersocietal

THE ACTION-CONCEPTS AS ORGANIZERS
OF THE CURRICULUM

The need for broad, generalized studies seems more urgent during the child's youthful period for he is in the process of acquiring the intellectual range that he will develop and bring to real depth in later years. Elementary studies are seen, therefore, as being organized around all six *action-concepts* at each grade level. The content and treatment is to become progressively more complex in a spiraling fashion. The topical input would be adjusted to the child's learning levels. Each of the six *action-concepts* would be treated in its own right but the interaction with the other concepts would be noted.

At the secondary level, one of the six *action-concepts* could be selected as the major focus of study for each grade level. There are also several possible alternatives to this arrangement. For instance, topics could be selected from a single discipline such as economics and the six *action-concepts* could be used as the inquiry tools; or a general topic such as the U.S. Constitution could be viewed from the perspective of the six concepts.

Two crucial points remain to be dealt with: In what way do the *action-concepts* achieve logical structuring of the curriculum? In what way can the learner make use of these *action-concepts* in confronting life situations? Each action-concept suggests a key question which is essential to the understanding of human behavior. In any given situation, these general questions could be used pedagogically to structure curriculum materials.

1. What conflicts exist in this situation?
2. How does power function in this situation?
3. How is valuing involved in this situation?
4. What are the stable interactions present in this situation (i.e., the traditions, the customs, the standards, the established relationships between institutions, etc.)?

5. What changes are occurring in this situation?
6. What adjustments are being made in this situation?

These are general questions which give the citizen an encompassing and reasonable way of dealing with the situations for which he must make decisions. Pedagogically, these questions suggest the avenues for inquiring into social situations, as well as the appropriate referents for information retrieval. Information pertaining to a situation can be organized around these questions. Generalizations and conclusions can be developed around these questions. Guided by these questions, the student and citizen may reach decisions and take courses of action.

Furthermore, the breakdown of each *action-concept* suggested in this work contributes to the study of a particular situation both in range and depth. For example, here are subquestions suggested by the analysis of *Conflict*.

1. What conflicts concerning goals are present within individuals and between individuals?
2. What conflicts concerning goals are present between individuals and institutions?
3. What conflicts concerning goals are present within institutions and between institutions?
4. What conflicts concerning goals are present within the society and between societies?
5. What conflicts in roles are present within individuals and between individuals?
6. In what ways do the means used in the situation contribute to conflict?

A similar procedure may be applied to each of the *action-concepts*.

Of course, the above subquestions do not refer to a specific content input. Once a topic is chosen, each of them could be developed in a number of more specific ways. Thus, it could be asked: "How did Johnny's desire to be a college track star conflict with his ambition to be a lawyer?" Or "Why did the school want Johnny to cut his hair?" The former question would lead to a discussion of intraindividual conflict, while the latter would lead to a discussion of individual-institutional conflict. In other words, it is not so much the wording of the question that is important (for this may vary depending on the topic), it is rather the usefulness of the categories under each *action-concept* for the achievement of completeness and logical structure that is important.

Moreover, it should be realized that not all the *action-concepts* or their accompanying questions are equally apropos of a given situation at a given time. Not all human behavior can be observed in a specific situation though it may well be latent. Thus, some questions will be more relevant under certain circumstances than under other circumstances. However, the *action-concepts* and their subconcepts do suggest search patterns for relationships not presently seen. For example, to take an extreme case, the relationship that might exist between wealth and the development of biological powers.

The kinds of questions which arise under the action-concepts can be used appropriately for both general topics and for more specialized topics such as the economic system or some portion of it as, e.g., the money system. Money could be analyzed from the perspective of *Power* and such questions could be raised as: "How is institutional authority represented by the money system?" "What are the traditions underlying our money system?" "In your judgment, is money more powerful than technological expertise and why?"

In a similar way, money could be analyzed from the perspective of *Valuing* or *Conflict*. For examples, questions could be raised concerning priority valuing. How has the importance attributed to the earning of money varied in present times, through history and among differing cultures? Put in other terms, how much value does the earning of money have for the individual and for society when compared to such things as time to enjoy nature, to participate in sports, etc.?

Furthermore, all of the preceding questions may be posed either for purposes of descriptive analyses or for purposes of evaluative analyses, i.e., they may be posed in the "what is . . ." form or in the "what should be . . ." form. The first is directed at ascertaining an existing state of affairs, while the second is directed at exploring or reaching decisions concerning more desirable future states of affairs.

As the study progresses, the pedagogical structure of the *action-concepts* is seen as being absorbed into the student's way of thinking. It is believed that this open-ended, but logical, structure will become the intellectual tools that can be made use of in any life situation. Ultimately, the student-citizen will use them quite naturally.

7 Pedagogical Media and the Curriculum Design

THE FUNCTION OF PEDAGOGICAL MEDIA IN SATISFYING THE ESTABLISHED CRITERIA

The goal of social studies—the raison d'être—is citizenship education. In a democratic society this can only mean that the citizen's models for significant decision making will be increased and refined. The sources of his models must be tapped over and over again so that truly relevant input for a social studies course may be achieved.

We have isolated seven major sources. These sources are not mutually exclusive, nor do they have a built-in logic. They have been discerned from life itself with its unpredictability and its multitude of modes of human behavior. There may be other valid sources for decision-making models which we have not perceived. There is no reason why these may not be added to the list established by us. The purpose of the list is to ensure that a sufficiently broad range of topics as well as a relevant range of topics will be dealt with in the schools. At present, subverbal impressions, exemplars, traditional beliefs, etc., are frequently overlooked while emphasis is placed on the social science disciplines. In this fashion, scholastic input misses the point of social studies, i.e., citizenship education and the improvement of significant decision-making models.

The presentation of *action-concepts* has been stimulated by the recognition of two basic requirements for the successful outcome of a social studies course: the need for content that is topical in nature and the need for curriculum structure which can reflect a logical ordering and thus serve as a valid organizer for the citizen's models. *Action-concepts* were chosen over concepts that were descriptive in a static sense, or solely prescriptive in nature, because of the range of their applicability which included both personal and societal concerns.

The selection of six *action-concepts* is, again, limited to the authors' abilities to discern the major ways of acting that occur within and between human societies. If additional *action-concepts* were perceived, presenting a unique quality of societal acting, while being sufficiently broad in scope as well as ahistorical in nature, there is no reason why such a concept or concepts could not be added to the list established. The effort, of course, was made to achieve a complete range of *action-concepts*.

By bringing the sources for topical input together with the categorization of *action-concepts*, most of the criteria set forth in Chapter 4 as vital to the construction of an adequate social studies curriculum are satisfied. The criteria which do not appear to be adequately satisfied as yet concern in-class treatment of the selected content. Open-endedness and flexibility in dealing with the specific

content selection, encouragement of students to generalize, and the requirement of active student involvement
are fundamental to the success of this curriculum plan
and means must be developed, curriculum-wise, which
insure the achievement of these characteristics.

Up to this point we have been clearly in the territory of
the curriculum planner. The in-class manipulation of specific content, the involvement of a student as a problem
solver and discoverer are factors which must depend
largely upon the teacher's abilities. A curriculum design
cannot predict the exact pupil membership or the particular learning characteristics of a class. The details of student involvement are teaching decisions. The teacher
serves as a pivot of flexibility between objective, overall
curriculum plans and the particular in-class situation.

Having said this, however, does not mean that the
curriculum planner cannot deal with the presentation of
materials in general terms. That is, he can present a
broad and continually changing range of pedagogical
media which will insure a variety of ways of thinking
about the content and of generalizing as well as the
different forms of student involvement. The teacher
would choose from a range of pedagogical media dealing
with specific content. Furthermore, the materials available would be so constructed that choice refers not only
to the selection of one or the other media but even to the
in-class usage of a selected media. Each presentation
would be devised in an open-ended fashion so that it
would be possible for the teacher to decide what portion
of the materials he wishes to use.

In other words, the effort would be to build into the
overall curriculum design the opportunities for "spur-of-
the-moment" decision making that is necessary if the
teacher is to be a pivot of flexibility between a highly
generalized curriculum design and the multitude of un-

predictable "goings-on" which characterize the average classroom. The use of a broad gamut of pedagogical media would be insured by its inclusion in long-ranged curriculum planning. A variety of media would become an actual part of the planned program rather than an inconsistent usage on the part of some teachers.

THE ELABORATION OF PEDAGOGICAL MEDIA

An effort to develop a series of pedagogical media particularly suited for topical input in a social studies course was undertaken. It was realized that any such list would never achieve completeness. New media are continually being invented. The purpose of creating a list was two-fold: to show the inherent possibilities and range of pedagogical media, and to enable the development of a sample scope and sequence chart covering a 1–12 social studies program.

Several psychological learning factors were necessarily kept in mind while the pedagogical media were being developed. The onset of abstract thinking abilities cannot be precisely pinpointed but the way children learn is fundamentally influenced by whether the abstract thinking stage has been attained. The differentiation between elementary and secondary materials was made primarily with this factor in mind.

The audio-visual media which seem most available to the average classroom are films, film strips, overhead slides, tapes, other types of recordings, and single pictures taken from magazines. Newspapers and books, though not ordinarily thought of as audio-visual techniques, are included in the group. The teaching techniques which seem most suited to the average classroom are posing problem situations, using original documents, treating current events *while they are still current*, and using comparisons which could range from a comparison of ideals and actions to a comparison of customs among different ethnic groups.

Audio-visual techniques and teaching techniques were interwoven to create a series of 14 pedagogical media, each of which was considered both suitable to treat topical content for any of the study areas indicated by the outlines of the six *action-concepts*, and sufficiently different to cause a different way of thinking in the student. Particular stress was placed on problems either involving the student in the actual solution or making the student seek the problem for which a solution is necessary. Problem involvement reflects most closely the decision-making situation of the citizen.

Descriptions of the 14 pedagogical media follow.

Inflammables

Inflammables would consist of a series of highly provocative and sometimes defiant questions to be presented to the students for their reactions. Particularly time-honored and traditional aspects of our culture would be subjects of such questions. For instance, students might be asked whether they were really so foolish as to think our Founding Fathers were moved primarily by a belief in freedom and equality. Why did most of them own slaves?

Inflammables, besides having a valid contribution to make in the development of thoughtful members of society, could also lead into a curriculum unit having as its subject the process of questioning. This unit could be divided into two parts. The first would deal with such types of questions as evaluative questions or questions for the acquisition of information. It would be quite brief and simplified for quick absorption on the secondary level. The subsequent phase would then take these core questions and, by use of adjectives, adverbs, or particular facts, would turn the questions into inflammables. The opposite process, i.e., making the questions favorable, would also be developed.

Loaded Headlines

A series of headlines, slanted or "loaded" in controversial directions, would be presented.

Where the headline is derived from an actual newspaper article, students would be requested to decide the facts that might accompany the headline, on the basis of the headline alone. Once their impressions had been verbalized, students would be requested to do some research in order to determine the facts that did accompany the headline. Citations for the research would be included in the teaching materials along with teaching suggestions. This form of the loaded-headlines technique would be directed to the secondary level.

Where the headline is fabricated rather than derived from a newspaper article, students would be requested to find or produce photographs that would interpret their understanding of the headline. Some adequate photos would be included in the teaching materials for teacher use when time is at a premium. However, there would be no right or wrong in the selection of pictures. The intention would be to aid the student in observing the convergent impressions derivable from a headline, and the reliability that may be attributed to such impressions. The student-selected pictures could serve as the subject of discussions and/or compositions and/or readings. This form of the loaded-headline technique would be directed to both primary and secondary levels. It seems particularly suited to the primary levels since the headlines could be fabricated with reference to childhood experiences and capacities.

Advertisements

One-page advertisements, similar to those praising the

fine qualities of some brand product but dealing with a pertinent social development, would be presented to students. At the secondary level, topics thus favorably advertised would range from communism to free enterprise, from labor unions to Ku Klux Klan. At the primary level, topics would relate more closely to childhood experiences. In this vein, motherhood or schools run by children might serve as subjects for advertisements. An advertisement might show, for instance, a very capable-looking little boy saying something to the effect that only children can really understand the needs of children and should therefore manage the schools.

Students would be asked to search for the pictorial and verbal "twists" which place the subject in an extremely favorable light. Meanings communicated without words would also be underscored. In the later grades, students would be asked to do research which would give a fuller understanding of the advertised topic, making it possible to note what unfavorable aspects might have been glossed over in the advertisement. Even younger children would be asked to scrutinize the advertisements with an eye to finding the rational weaknesses.

A related exercise would involve students actively participating in the production of advertisements concerning topics of social importance. Ideas and techniques for producing such advertisements would be included in the curriculum materials for the teacher's reference. Ways of relating these to the *action-concepts* and to the other curriculum materials would also be included.

Audio-Experiences

Audio-experiences are dramatic presentations, either taped or recorded, dealing with one or more aspects of an *action-concept*. On the preabstract level they would make considerable use of fantasy. While logical explanations of concepts would be presented, the precise understanding of such logic would not be pivotal to the learning situation. Often the young child is able to work effectively with the operations involved in a situation without completely comprehending the underlying logic. This is the case with the child's native tongue. The use of fantasy makes it possible to be less insistent on logical comprehension while permitting major problems to be examined or, at least, opened to future questioning. Problem situations would be the type of content employed. The solutions to these problems, i.e., the endings to the stories, would be included at the primary level. On the secondary level, the situations would be more realistic, with incomplete, open-ended plots entailing a considerable amount of logical analysis.

Problem Posers

Brief, filmed episodes lasting not more than three or four minutes would present current events in the form of problem situations. By means of these situations, students could identify with the issues. The problem situation would be left unresolved and students would be requested to seek a variety of possible solutions. Several filmed solutions would be included in the materials for the students to view after they have reached their own conclusions so that they would have the opportunity of reviewing and evaluating their own solutions.

  Problem posers need not be filmed; they could be presented in prose form. It would, however, be more desirable in the lower grades if the question of reading skills were not placed between the young child and consideration of the issues of his environment. The grade level of materials would be determined primarily by the complexity and abstractness of the problem situations presented.

Documents

Students would be presented with original documents regarding a subject with which they have already come in contact. Human rights might be such a subject. For example, documents concerning human rights, issued by committees of the United Nations, might be carefully studied with the aim of investigating what had and had not been included. Comparisons would then be made with other documents dealing with the same subject, such as the recent "Mankind Declaration" prepared by Quincy Wright for the Council for the Study of Mankind, Inc.

Controversial areas would also be the object of the presentation of original documents. The background of controversies would be quickly sketched in for students. Then the original documents would be supplied and students would be asked to judge for themselves. Controversies and original documents used in the early grades would be realistic but mostly imaginary so as to fit the particular learning characteristics of the young child. By the third or fourth grade, originals would be introduced.

Pen Products

This medium would view literary production in historical and cultural perspective. Topics or events, which have been the objects of novels, short stories, plays, and the like, would be studied through their literary productions as well as through a simple listing of the most undisputed facts. The variations in interpretations, the omissions of some and not other aspects, the imaginative input of different authors, the historical problems that remain to be solved, etc., would become an integral part of the study. For instance, "Authority" could be studied by a comparison of the pen products concerning the United States Constitutional Convention. Among the works that could be reviewed are the Broadway musical hit, *1776,* and various biographies of the most famous adversaries at the Convention. Another possibility would be the study of the ideal home life as a form of *Interaction.* Home life could be studied in different eras as well as in the present era. *Life with Father,* a comic strip such as "Blondie," and a family situation TV production could serve as pen products and as sources of comparison. The question of dynamic *Change* could also be developed in such a unit.

Coupled Pictures

Coupled pictures would utilize the visual image to bring about understanding of and linkage between pertinent phenomena of societal development which might otherwise require long pages of explanation. For instance, the coupling of a picture of a new-born and therefore helpless baby with the picture of a full-grown, well-armed policeman could lead to a discussion not only of how man biologically acquires powers by which he can control some of his world, but of how he has learned to increase these powers by the use of instruments. Furthermore, some instruments acquire symbolic power. This is the case with the policeman's gun which represents governmental authority—another form of power.

Coupled pictures having obvious contrasts or logical sequence would be used for both the primary and secondary levels. These would be especially dramatic and contain references easily related to personal or current events so that they could serve as focal points of class discussions. Photographs representing more abstract and complexly linked societal concepts would be included in secondary curriculum packets. For instance, the picture of a little black girl holding a white doll and a picture of a defiant, wildly bushy-haired black woman would be presented in the effort to lead a class into examining rising black power and the continual domination in a

black youth's life of white culture, symbolically represented by the white baby doll.

Flashes

A series of slides, ranging from 10 to 15 in number, would
be flashed on a screen. Each slide would be viewed for no
more than a few seconds. The series would build around
some topic of human concern fraught with emotion such
as poverty, prejudice, war, or strikes. The flashes are
intended to make the students more aware of their own
affective responses to such emotion-laden topics. The
students might be asked which of the slides most im-
pressed them. The slides could be shown again. What do
they sense about poverty from the photos viewed? What
about the bum sleeping against a building wall in the
street? Students could produce flashes of their own, and
be asked to explain and justify their creations. In this
regard they could be asked to do research, sift facts, and
come to conclusions.

Primary children could be introduced to flashes by
using a series which would remain within the most familiar theaters of life. Gang fights and poor urban schools
might make interesting and comprehensible series for
both the upper and lower grades.

News Photos

One means of "loading" or slanting an article of the mass
media is by use of the photograph. News photos would be
presented to students separately from the articles they
accompanied. Students would be asked to speculate about
the contents of the magazine or newspaper articles on
the basis of the photos. The full-length article would then
be studied. Interested students could try to produce more
"equitable" photographs for the articles.

Photographs are carriers not only of misleading conceptions, but of societal meanings that are often unconsciously accepted within the framework of an article. A

search for such connotations, unconscious contradictions, and misconceptions would be a major objective with the use of this technique. Primary students might collect news photos into a series called, "Photos of Our Times." At the upper grade levels, the photos could be brought together with brief paragraphs indicating the insights gained through the separate analysis of the photos and then their subsequent combination with the original articles.

Lyrical Patterns

The lyrics of songs, popular either through the ages of one culture or contemporarily in different cultures, would be brought together as carriers of topical input. Recordings of the songs along with individual printouts of the song lyrics would be included in the curriculum materials. Topics might include: Songs of the Urban Culture; Songs of the Patriot; Songs of Man and Nature; Songs of War; Songs of Love; etc. The words and expressions used repeatedly in different cultures or eras would be examined. Recurring themes would be compared for changes in treatment. The kind of music accompanying the lyrics would also be examined. The attempt would be to increase understanding of a particular culture or period through the popular expression of song. Questions regarding the nature of *Power, Change, Interaction,* etc., would be posed for student consideration in relationship to one or another group of songs.

Students could be encouraged to write their own songs in the different topic areas with particular emphasis on the present. Class members could analyze the lyrical content of the student productions.

Clichés

Sayings, linguistic expressions based on habit or tradition or derived from poems, faddish slang, and other clichés would be presented. Comic strips would be one of the chief sources of such clichés for the primary grades. If "Priscilla's Pop" says, "It's the early bird that gets the worm," or, "Haste makes waste," in a Sunday comic strip, the strip would be presented in its entirety. The clichés would be pointed out and the pupils would be asked to examine the truth and validity of these expressions. For more mature primary children, contradictory or inconsistent groups of sayings would also be presented. Besides comic strips, magazines, newspapers, and popular books would serve as source materials for clichés.

The presentation of clichés would continue on the secondary level with political, economic, and sociological writings becoming the major sources. In addition to habitual expressions, pivotal words such as "inflation" and "buying power" would be examined in historical perspective in order to determine whether the actual meanings of such words have remained stable or have undergone change which is not really represented or taken into account under certain conditions of usage.

Role Productions

A pertinent situation of historical, sociological, or political importance would be presented to the students. Photographs and dramatic accounts of supporting details, either imaginative or factual, would be included so that an image of the situation would be created within the students' minds. They would be familiarized with the beginning, middle, and end of the situation. Then, each student would be assigned a role and requested to create a part for himself as a participant in the unfolding drama. The reasons for doing what was done in the situation should become clear through the dialogue. Students holding different roles would consult with each other to see how they would react to the dialogues of the others. If the situation is an historically true situation, students could do research, read biographies, etc.

Personality Constructs

Universal human phenomena would be viewed in cultural perspective. The satisfaction of fundamental human needs such as the acquisition of alimentation, reproduction, and socialization would be noted and the student's imagination would be employed in describing the characteristics of personalities that might be reinforced by one and not another culture, by one and not another environment, by one and not another government. Aspects of *Interaction* could be developed with considerable perspective by means of such a technique.

Among related exercises would be a review of the six *action-concepts* to determine which had been emphasized in the different personality descriptions. Another related exercise would be furnishing students with descriptions of personality traits and asking them to describe the type of culture that might favor such traits. Of course, in the selection of types there would be no right answers. Consistency in the answers would, however, be sought.

In the primary grades the human needs examined could be held at their simplest level. For instance, hunger might be conveyed by the way children are nursed. In one culture, the nursing child finds his mother's nipple pulled away and left just out of his reach. In another, he is nursed by means of a sterilized bottle.

In the secondary grades, the human needs examined would be at the more complex levels. The question of salary as a means of satisfying needs could be typified in a number of differing cultures. The major purpose of the personality construct would be to underline the ongoing interaction between the individual and his culture.

For practical purposes, the number of pedagogical media used in a school term might have to be decreased to permit more class time for the in-depth study of each

unit. The shorter attention span and the need for continual variation at the elementary levels makes a large
number of teaching approaches particularly useful. With
the increase in the student's attention span and with the
thrust toward the more in-depth study of each *action-
concept*, it was felt that the number of pedagogical media
used should be reduced. For this purpose the pedagogical
media have been grouped according to similarities either
of audio-visual approach or teaching technique. Thus, one
pedagogical medium could be selected from each group,
thereby retaining a variety in the media to be used. The
following groupings were somewhat arbitrarily decided
upon. There is no reason why different pedagogical media
could not be devised. Nor is there any reason why the
grouping of techniques could not follow some other
means of selection. For that matter, students at the secondary level could begin to develop their own media.

Inflammables Loaded headlines Advertisements	Newspaper media
Audio-experiences Problem posers	Dramatic media (involving problem solving)
Documents Pen products	Historical-research media
Coupled pictures Flashes News photos	Photographic media
Lyrical patterns Clichés	Semantic media (past, present, and intercultural)

Role production
Personality constructs   Media for psychological-
        and   sociological
Media developed by   involvement
    students

Packets of materials are envisioned which would make use of several different media to treat topics within the scope of each of the six *action-concepts*. The manipulation of pedagogical media has no real significance if the guiding criteria for their use is not kept in mind. The media are no more than empty mechanisms unless they present content so that it remains open-ended and flexible at the classroom level, and unless such media encourage generalizations and actively involve the student.

The expectations arising from the formats of the materials to be studied are of vital importance. If the answers are all known beforehand, the type of decision making developed in the student will not be significant. The student will simply be learning to adapt his decisions to the expected "right" answers. The goal of increasing the significant decision-making powers of the citizen can best be served by materials that indicate various avenues of thought rather than absolute answers. Teachers, of course, will have some answers—their answers—which will no doubt be useful to students surveying alternatives. However, the student must be expected to search for his own answer, to substitute previously reached conclusions with improved models not just once, but over and over again.

8 Putting the Parts Together: Scope and Sequence

A three-pronged sequence for curriculum development has been proposed. The first phase involves a search for relevant, current topics derived from the sources for the citizen's decision-making models. Seven categories based on the origins of these models have been established. During the social studies course, topics should be derived from all seven categories.

The second phase involves viewing the selected topics through an *action-concept* (or action-concepts). The *action-concepts* have been developed as an educational means of organizing the study of what men do in their life together. The six *action-concepts* selected present a complete range of the actions occurring both individually and societally. A sufficiently broad social studies course would therefore not only deal with topics derived from

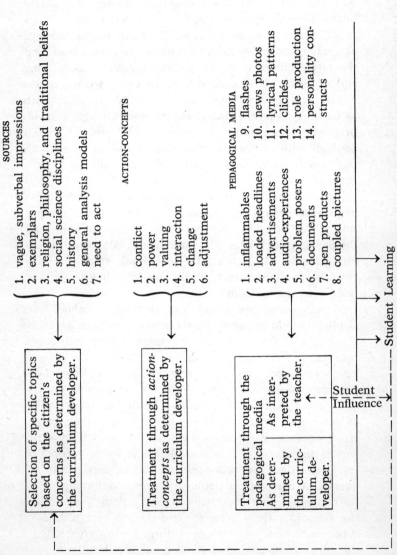

SOURCES

1. vague, subverbal impressions
2. exemplars
3. religion, philosophy, and traditional beliefs
4. social science disciplines
5. history
6. general analysis models
7. need to act

ACTION-CONCEPTS

1. conflict
2. power
3. valuing
4. interaction
5. change
6. adjustment

PEDAGOGICAL MEDIA

1. inflammables
2. loaded headlines
3. advertisements
4. audio-experiences
5. problem posers
6. documents
7. pen products
8. coupled pictures
9. flashes
10. news photos
11. lyrical patterns
12. clichés
13. role production
14. personality constructs

Selection of specific topics based on the citizen's concerns as determined by the curriculum developer.

Treatment through *action-concepts* as determined by the curriculum developer.

Treatment through the pedagogical media As determined by the curriculum developer. | As interpreted by the teacher.

→ Student Learning

Student Influence

The student, as a citizen, is also a source of input

all seven sources for decision-making models, but would insure that all sources would be treated from the perspective of each *action-concept*. The former offers a range of study comparable to the students' life experiences, and the latter offers a comprehensive means of classifying and ordering these experiences. In other words, topics under the category, "Need to act," should be dealt with as *Conflict, Power, Valuing, Interaction, Change,* and *Adjustment;* topics under the category, *"Exemplars"* should be dealt with as *Conflict, Power,* etc.; and so on until all the sources have been treated through all the action-concepts.

The third phase involves implementing the decisions made with regard to specific input through the production of packets of curriculum materials which would use the pedagogical media. The number of pedagogical media may be reduced for the sake of in-depth study. The diagram below summarizes the three interacting phases and their constituent members.

As was noted previously, the elementary school curriculum would present all six *action-concepts* at every grade level. Topics would be tapped from all seven sources, but a complete rotation of topics and sources every term would not be necessary. The secondary school program would select one of the six *action-concepts* for study during the school year, and would use that concept as the major organizing factor in the study of topics derived from the seven sources for decision-making models.

It is unnecessary at either the primary or secondary levels for the *action-concepts* to follow a particlar sequence. A bank of curriculum packets containing materials and teaching ideas should be available, and either the school or the teachers could determine which concepts and which materials would most adequately satisfy the needs of their students at a particular level.

The sequencing of materials according to learning ability would occur not only among the separate packets of materials but within each packet, and would involve the teacher's judgment. The complexity of materials included in a packet would span several grades of the elementary or secondary levels. The teacher would select the materials in a packet according to the maturity of his class. Fewer of the materials at the abstract level of thought might be selected for a slower group, while all or only the most complex of the materials might be selected for a more advanced group.

At the elementary level, curriculum packets would be classified under the *action-concepts*. Thus, a complete term-long social studies course would consist of six packets. Each packet would develop topics from several sources and would employ several pedagogical media. At the secondary level, packets would be classified according to the subdivisions outlined in the analysis of each *action-concept*. For instance, if the *action-concept* selected for a year-long study were *Conflict*, the packets developed might be: "Goal Conflicts: Individual and Institutional," "Goal Conflicts: Institutional and Societal," "Role Conflicts," and "Instrumental Conflicts." Each packet would deal with several topics derived from the sources and would employ several pedagogical media. Ideally, more than one packet of materials for each area of study would be available permitting a wider choice with regard to the topical input and the pedagogical media used. This would also permit zeroing in on one or the other of the sources. A study of economics could be developed through *Power* or some other *action-concept*. Exemplars could be treated with greater depth from the perspective of "Goal Conflicts." The curriculum bank should present more materials than the teacher would ordinarily use so that the teacher has an effective choice to make from among its offerings.

If a curriculum bank for the proposed social studies program had curriculum packets involving the complete rotation of the seven sources, the six *action-concepts* and all 14 pedagogical media, there would be 588 different presentations of materials for each of the elementary grades. Obviously, such a quantity of production is prohibitive. This high number of areas of study would, nevertheless, not interfere with a reasonably close administrative check concerning what had been studied, how it had been studied and, within a span of a few semesters, when it was planned for study. Even though no particular grade assignment has been given to the *action-concepts*, a scope and sequence chart is useful for a within-grade development as well as for an overall view of what has been or will be accomplished.

The proposed scope and sequence chart is envisioned primarily as a checklist and will hereafter be called "scope and sequence checklist" to emphasize this function.

The scope and sequence checklist would aid not only in ascertaining whether the entire range of sources, *action-concepts*, and pedagogical media had been tapped,

Phase I. Scope and Sequence Checklist: Elementary Level

| Action-concepts | Sources* | | | | | | |
	A	B	C	D	E	F	G
Power–1	1A	1B	1C	1D	1E	1F	1G
Conflict–2	2A	2B	2C	2D	2E	2F	2G
Valuing–3	3A	3B	3C	3D	3E	3F	3G
Interaction–4	4A	4B	4C	4D	4E	4F	4G
Change–5	5A	5B	5C	5D	5E	5F	5G
Adjustment–6	6A	6B	6C	6D	6E	6F	6G

*A = Value, subverbal sources
 B = Exemplars
 C = Religion, philosophy, and traditional beliefs
 D = Social science disciplines
 E = History
 F = General analysis models
 G = Need to act

Phase II. Scope and Sequence Checklist: Elementary Level

Pedagogical Media	Interaction Sources and Action-Concepts																					
	1A	2A	3A	4A	5A	6A	1B	2B	3B	4B	5B	6B	1C	2C	3C	4C	5C	6C	1D	2D	3D	Etc.
Inflammables																						
Loaded headlines																						
Advertisements																						
Audio-experiences																						
Problem posers																						
Documents																						
Pen products																						
Coupled pictures																						
Flashes																						
News photos																						
Lyrical patterns																						
Clichés																						
Role production																						
Personality constructs																						

Phase I.   Scope and Sequence Checklist: Secondary Level

Action-concept	Sources*						
Conflict	A	B	C	D	E	F	G
Goal conflict inter-intraindividual–1	1A	1B	1C	1D	1E	1F	1G
Goal conflict inter-intrainstitutional–2	2A	2B	2C	2D	2E	2F	2G
Goal conflict inter-intrasocietal–3	3A	3B	3C	3D	3E	3F	3G
Role conflict intra-individual–4	4A	4B	4C	4D	4E	4F	4G
Role conflict inter-individual–5	5A	5B	5C	5D	5E	5F	5G
Instrumental conflict–6	6A	6B	6C	6D	6E	6F	6G

*A = Value subverbal sources
B = Exemplars
C = Religion, philosophy, and traditional beliefs
D = Social science disciplines
E = History
F = General analysis models
G = Need to act

Phase II. Scope and Sequence Checklist: Secondary Level

Pedagogical Media	Interaction Sources and Conflict									
	1A	2A	3A	4A	5A	6A	1B	2B	3B	Etc.
Newspaper media										
Dramatic media										
Historical-research media										
Semantic media										
Psychological-sociological involvement										
Photographic media										
Student-developed media										

but also in the choice and manipulation of curriculum packets so that sequencing would be adapted to the needs of a particular population. If the present trend continues and an increasing number of schools adopt modular scheduling and the use of computer machines for class organization, the manipulations necessary to keep track of what has and has not been studied by each student would be reduced to a simple computer program.

At the initial phases of the proposed curriculum, it is not only possible but advisable that the number of areas for study be reduced to more manageable proportions. The inherent flexibility of the design enables such reductions. We have already noted that at the elementary level, each *action-concept* would be concerned with only *several* of the sources and would use only *several* media. However, for the sake of using the most difficult of examples, the scope and sequence checklists on pages 116, 117 will represent one elementary school year with the 588 study areas that would occur if the sources, *action-concepts*, and media were completely rotated. The checklist is divided into two phases. Phase I plots the interaction of sources and *action-concepts*. Phase II plots the interaction of pedagogical media with the completed interaction of sources and *action-concepts*. This second phase presents a 42×14 checklist.

The scope and sequence checklists at the secondary level would look considerably different since only one *action-concept* and its subdivisions would be interacting with the sources and the pedagogical media. The pedagogical media themselves would be reduced in number so that a more extended and in-depth study of each subdivision can be undertaken. Essentially, however, the twin phases of the scope and sequence checklist would operate in a fashion similar to those of the elementary checklist.

9 Sample Materials for an Open Social Studies Curriculum

As curriculum planners, we felt the urge to illustrate our design with some materials which could be used in the schools. Unless materials can be successfully produced and introduced in the schools, our ideas, like the many that have preceded them, will have lost without a fight to the predominating subject curriculum.

To develop entire curriculum packets would be well beyond the scope of this initial effort. However, it was felt that the inclusion of two elements for an elementary school packet as well as two elements for a secondary school packet would be feasible.

EXAMPLES OF MATERIALS FOR
THE ELEMENTARY SCHOOL

Element I for a Curriculum Packet on *Power*

Grade level: Third (with possible use in the second and fourth grades).

Source for topical input: Need to act; vague subverbal impressions.

Action-concept: Power—biological power in the sense of physical, mental, and emotional characteristics; possession in the sense of property; religious power in the mythological sense; authority; groupness; and individual expertise. While *Power* is the focus of this element, *Conflict, Valuing,* and *Adjustment* are also involved.

Pedagogical media: Audio-experience (time of recording approximately four minutes). Script to be included for teacher study.

Audio-Experience title: "Jeffrey Genie: The Genie of Power"

MUSIC: Exotic and somewhat mysterious. Fades under and out.

JEFFREY GENIE: *(Pert, high-pitched voice heard through an echo chamber.)* Come in. Come into my bottle. There's only one day a year that I can have guests. So come in and keep me company.

MUSIC: Very brief, rising music so as to create the illusion of a musical question mark.

JEFFREY GENIE: Hmmm . . . maybe my bottle is too tiny for you. But you can listen. Not much has happened today. No one has picked my bottle up, or asked for anything. My name's Jeffrey. I'm the genie of power . . . oh . . . oh, my bottle's going upside down . . . oh. . . .

MUSIC: From under, very excited, and jumbled.

SOUND: A bottle bouncing on hard ground without break-
     ing.
JEFFREY GENIE: That was a terrible upset. That was like
     rolling off a mountain top, or being kicked by a
     horse. Maybe I can see outside my bottle. The glass
     is so dirty.
SOUND: Huffing on the glass with subsequent rubbing as
     if to clean.
JEFFREY: It looks like we're in a city dump, or an empty
     lot of some sort. There's a little boy lying on the
     ground. Poor kid. His head is bleeding. I wonder if
     he's dead. He's moving. I think he's all right. *(Ex-
     cited.)* I hope he picks me up and asks for some-
     thing. *(Happily).* That's his hand . . . reaching for
     me. . . .
SOUND: Glass bottle being drawn against rough ground.
JIM: *(Voice is muffled and distant.)* I wish I were big and
     strong. I'd show 'em.   *(Power:* physical)
SOUND AND MUSIC: Small, puff-like explosion mingled with
     climatic music.
N.B. The voices of both Jim and Jeffrey are now heard
normally.
JIM: Wow. There must be something wrong with my
     head. A bottle can't turn into a man—a midget at
     that.
JEFFREY GENIE: Thanks for calling me out of my bottle,
     but please don't call me a man—or a midget.
JIM: Well . . . what are you?
JEFFREY GENIE: *(Proudly.)* I'm Jeffrey Genie, the genie of
     power. I can do many things that men, midgets,
     and even giants can't do. *(Power:* mythological)
JIM: Can you turn trees into money?
JEFFREY GENIE: No, I can't do that.
JIM: Can you turn a pumpkin into a carriage?
JEFFREY GENIE: No, I can't do that.

JIM: Can you fix my head up so it won't bleed any more?

JEFFREY GENIE: I'm afraid not.

JIM: Well, what can you do then?

JEFFREY GENIE: I told you. I'm the genie of power.

JIM: "Power?" What's that good for? I mean, what can you do with it?

JEFFREY GENIE: Anything *you* can do, I can give you more power to do it with. That means you will be able to do it better than other people can do it. All kids can run. But now that my bottle is in your hands, if you ask me for the power to run fast, I can make you the fastest runner in the world.

(*Power*: physical)

JIM: Can you give me the power to fight better?

JEFFREY GENIE: I suppose I could make you the best fighter in the world, if that's what you want. But why would you want that?

JIM: (*Holding back the tears.*) Look at me. They beat me up, and all I wanted to do was play in this lot.

(*Conflict:* interindividual goal)

JEFFREY GENIE: Who are "they"?

JIM: The Black Hawks. They don't own this lot any more than I do, but they're the biggest, strongest kids in the neighborhood. Everybody's too scared to even come near here.

(*Power:* possession, groupness, physical)

JEFFREY GENIE: You're not very big or strong. Why did you come here?

JIM: The kids on my block were playing stickball. I don't play very well, so nobody wanted me on their team. Mom's out working and . . . I don't know . . . I just wanted something to do. I came here to play with the old rubber tire that Larry is always bouncing around. The lot was empty, but Larry caught me.   (*Power:* expertise)

JEFFREY GENIE: Who's Larry?

JIM: He's one of the Hawks. But I don't think he wanted to beat me up.

JEFFREY GENIE: Why did he then?

JIM: He tried to get me to leave before the other Hawks saw me, but I didn't want to run like a sissy. The Big Chief of the Hawks said that if they were soft and would let anyone play in their lot, pretty soon it wouldn't be theirs. I said I wouldn't come back and Larry didn't want to hit me. But the Big Chief got tough and told Larry and another guy that they'd better beat me up, or else. *(Crying.)* So they started to punch me. I ran away and someone threw you, uh . . . I mean your bottle at me.
                    (*Power:* possession, authority)

JEFFREY GENIE: I really couldn't help hitting you. But I can give you the power of strength so that you'd be so strong you could beat anyone up.

JIM: Can you really do that for me?

JEFFREY GENIE: Sure, just put me in your back pocket. As long as I'm there, you'll be the strongest boy in the world.   (*Power:* mythological)

MUSIC: A whisking whistle into crescendo music, brief and cut.

JIM: Gee, I can feel my muscles getting bigger. I feel strong all over. Let's see how high I can bounce this tire now.

SOUND: Bouncing "plop" of tire.

LARRY: You must be nuts, kid, to be playing in this lot. When the Big Chief threw that bottle at you we thought you were dead. That's why we ran away.

JIM: Well I'm not going to be the dead guy anymore. Why don't you try and stop me from playing with your tire, Larry?   (*Conflict:* interindividual goal)

LARRY: I don't have to. Here come some of my friends— Hawks.   (*Power:* physical, groupness)

SOUND: Several boys running across the lot, progressively closer.

BIG CHIEF: Let's beat him to a pulp this time. We were too soft the first time around. You, too, Larry.

SOUND: Vehement fighting among four or five fellows.

JIM: *(Puffing and panting.)* Let's see who owns this lot now.   *(Power:* possession; physical)

SOUND: Grunts and groans. Big Chief screams.

BIG CHIEF: Let's get out of here.

SOUND: Boys running away, fade and out. Silence except for Jim's heavy puffing.

JIM: Go on and run. Sissies. I showed 'em. *(Pause.)* I guess this lot's mine now. *(Enthusiastically.)* Gosh, look at that old bed. The springs still look good.

SOUND: Jumping up and down on bedspring. Cut.

JIM: Whoops . . . I wish some of the other kids could see me now. *(Pause.)* I wonder whose tea kettle this was. It has a hole in it.

SOUND: A couple of flute-like sounds.

JIM: But it can still whistle. *(Wistfully.)* Gee, I wish there were some kids around.

MUSIC: A whisking whistle into crescendo music, brief and cut.

JEFFREY GENIE: Why did you pull me out of your pocket? I thought we were doing pretty well. Now you're a weakling again.   *(Power:* mythological; physical)

JIM: Aw . . . I don't want to be the strongest boy in the world. It isn't any more fun beating people up than being beat up. I don't want this lot if there aren't any people on it.

                    (Valuing: priority valuing, ahistorical)

JEFFREY GENIE: Well, power doesn't only mean beating people up, or running faster than other kids do. You could ask for the power of imagination if you'd like.   *(Power:* mental)

JIM: What's that?

JEFFREY GENIE: With the power of imagination you can think of all sorts of things to do or make. That old tire could become a circus lady's hoop. It could even be a swing if you hung it from a tree. And story after story would come into your head. Do you understand?

JIM: *(Doubtful.)* I guess so. But you could have the best imagination in the world and still not have anyone to play with. I don't like being alone.

(*Valuing:* priority valuing, ahistorical)

JEFFREY GENIE: Well, then, why don't you ask for the power of friendship? Everyone would want to be your friend—and through you they could become friends with each other.   (*Power:* emotional)

JIM: *(In amazement.)* You mean, there's the power of friendship, too?

JEFFREY GENIE: Sure. People don't only do things because they're afraid. Sometimes they do things because they want to be together with each other.

JIM: That's what I want—the power of friendship.

MUSIC: A whisking whistle into crescendo music, brief and out.

JIM: My muscles aren't very big any more, but I feel happy all over. That's Big Chief across the street. *(Shouting.)* Hey, Big Chief . . . Big Chief.

BIG CHIEF: Don't . . . hit me any more. I won't come into your lot, honest.   (*Adjustment:* interindividual)

JIM: But I want you to come and play in the lot.

BIG CHIEF: You mean, you'd let me play in the lot?

JIM: Sure, Big Chief. I don't want to fight any more.

(*Adjustment:* interindividual)

BIG CHIEF: Would you let Larry and some of the other guys play here too?

JIM: Sure, I would. Only . . . no one would be boss. I mean, we wouldn't have a big chief.

(*Adjustment:* individual-institutional)

BIG CHIEF: I guess I'm not much of a big chief now.

SOUND: High, shrill whistle.

BIG CHIEF: They'll hear that and come running.

SOUND: Group of boys running, cut.

LARRY: *(Puffing.)* Hey, he's here. I thought you were going to give the all-clear when he was gone. My head hurts so much. I can't fight anymore.

JIM: We don't have to fight. Let's be friends.

LARRY: *(Sneering)*. Friends until I try to play with *my* tire.

JIM: We could take turns playing with it. If you want to be friends with me the way I want to be friends with you, we'll find a way.

> (*Adjustment:* interindividual)

LARRY: You know, kid, I like you. What's your name?

JIM: Jim.

BIG CHIEF: And my name's Charlie. There's not going to be a big chief of the Black Hawks anymore.

JIM: I'm so happy. I just gotta jump on this bed a little. Look.

SOUND: Jumping up and down on bedsprings. Fade into music.

MUSIC: A whisking whistle into crescendo music, brief and under.

JEFFREY GENIE: *(Voice passes from normal reproduction into echo chamber.)* Oh . . . Oh . . . Jim, I'm falling . . . Now he can't hear me. I'm back in my bottle. Who knows who'll pick me up next time, or what kind of power will be asked for.

END OF SCRIPT

TEACHING SUGGESTIONS

A *discussion* following the end of the recording might evolve around any or all of the following questions and accompanying annotations.

1. What kinds of power did the Genie and Jim talk

about? (*Annotation:* running fast; fighting well; turning things into other things such as trees into money; healing such as Jimmy's bleeding head; owning things such as the city lot; imagination; friendship.)

2. Are there other kinds of power? (*Annotation:* This is an open-ended question that could go just about anywhere. For instance, "writing" is a form of power because it permits man to communicate across the centuries: It enables him to store information and retrieve it when he needs it. A "pleasant personality" will often achieve goals where physical force will fail. A doctor's pills used to heal a patient is another example, and so forth.)

3. Why did the kids want a club like the Black Hawks? Would you like to belong to a club? What kind of a club would you like to belong to? (*Annotation:* "Club" may be likened to society or explained as a means of increasing biological power. People value being with other people. They also value being more powerful. Several boys together are certainly stronger than one boy alone.)

4. Why wasn't Jimmy satisfied? Would you have been satisfied? (*Annotation:* A discusion of human needs could be undertaken. If a man is hungry and another man can give him food, the man with food has power over the man without food. The way power functions reflects the way men's needs are satisfied. Jimmy's need for friendship and for something to do were not being satisfied in the existing power situation.)

5. Is friendship really a human need? Could man do without other men? (*Annotation:* No one could really answer this question. Much depends on what is meant by a human being. If a man could not talk, if he did not write, etc., would he still be a human being? What would he be? These are value questions related to the needs of men and the way power functions. If men believe they need friendship, friendship will be a source of power. Hopefully the children will be left perplexed by the dis-

cussion which could be personalized by asking the children whether they could do without other people.)

6. Did what happened to Jim remind you of anything that happened to you? Does everybody want and like you? Have you ever been pushed around? What did it feel like to be pushed around? (*Annotation:* These are very personal questions concerning how power has functioned in the lives of the students, and it would be best if the children began to ask each other questions about the incidents they recount. The teacher would primarily indicate who or what was using "power" in the incident described. He might then ask the class to judge whether those who were using "power" in the incidents were using it fairly.)

Activities for Children to Do

1. Several children could be assigned the roles of the characters in "Jeffrey Genie: The Genie of Power." Each could try to explain why he did what he did. The Chief of the Black Hawks would defend his use of power and even Jeffrey might explain why he did not help Jim to make a better choice in asking for power. The class would act as judges, asking questions and giving their opinions.

2. Some research on urban gangs could be undertaken. The Mafia, Clans, and so forth might be looked into. Why do they use their power the way they do?

3. Either individually or as a class, another story about the use of power could be written. This story could be based on the children's real-life experiences.

Element II for a Curriculum Packet on *Power*

Grade level: Third (with possible use in the second and fourth grades).

Source for topical input: Social science disciplines (political science); vague Subverbal Impressions; traditional beliefs.

Action-concept: Power—biological power in the sense of physical and mental characteristics; posession in the sense of tools; institutional and traditional authority; and groupness. While *Power* is the focus of this element, *Conflict* and *Valuing* are also referred to.

Pedagogical media: Coupled pictures. (The pictures to be presented to the pupils are on pages 132–133.)

TEACHING SUGGESTIONS

(*Note:* Neither the sequences nor all the phases suggested here must be followed for any one of the teaching ideas included to be successful.)

1. Present the photo of the newborn child and ask pupils to describe what they see. A comparison of the adult hands that are holding the child and the child's own weak legs could be very effectively made. (*Power:* physical.)

2. Present the photo of the well-armed policeman and have the pupils compare this picture with that of the baby. In particular, a comparison of the policeman's sturdy arms might be made with those of the child, and consequently used to develop the concept of biological power acquired through growth. The pupils might then be invited to observe the arms of all the members of the class. Do all people have equally strong arms, legs, imagination, memory, etc.? (*Power:* physical; mental)

3. Instruments that might be held by the policeman, such as a nightstick and handcuffs, could be pointed out to the pupils. The following questions might be asked: Why is the policeman carrying a gun? What can he do with a gun that he cannot do without it? If two boys were equally matched, what could the effect of the possession of a stick be? The teacher might attempt to guide the class to realize that such instruments are man's means of extending and increasing his physical power. This power

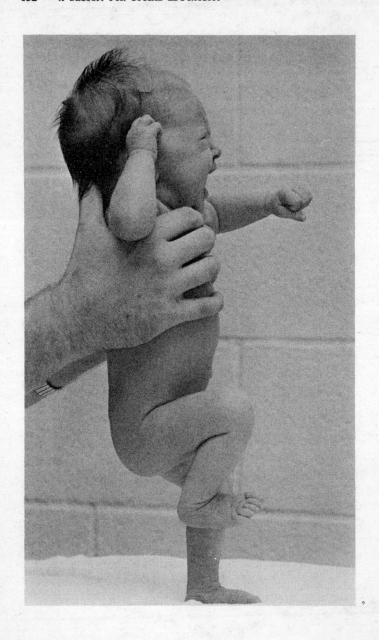

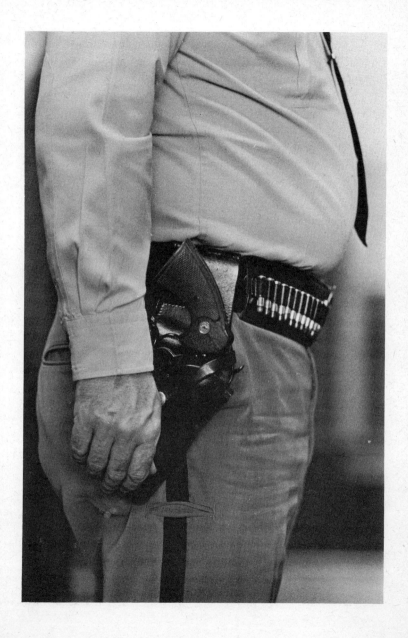

may be exercised over other men or over the environment in general (*Power:* tools)

4. What other instruments does man use to extend his power?

Annotation

Electric light enables man to extend his visual power by permitting him to see in the dark. (*Power:* tools.)

Jet airplane enables man to fly (a power which birds possess biologically) and to move at speeds far beyond his biological capacity. (*Power:* tools; individual expertise)

Typewriter enables man to write more quickly and clearly than his hands are capable of doing. (*Power:* tools; individual expertise.)

Alphabet enables man to communicate with others even when he is not present. (*Power:* mental; tools; individual expertise; institutional expertise.)

Hammer enables man to hit harder and with more accuracy than he could with any part of his body. (*Power:* physical; tools; individual expertise.)

5. Instruments, because they are carriers of particular kinds of power, also become symbols of authority in the society. What do the nightstick and the handcuffs represent? The gun is less symbolic. Why? (*Power:* traditional authority; institutional authority) What is brought to mind by each of the following:

Parking meter	Gavel
Ambulance siren	Crane
Desk and typewriter	

Do they extend power? Do they make you think of some kind of power? Which of them are most symbolic?

Annotation

Instruments become less symbolic as they are used by more and more people and as they are used to accomplish more and more acts. Thus, a desk and typewriter are the least symbolic since anyone from the President of the United States to an average student might use these to write a letter or study or even doodle. The crane is associated with building. The parking meter is symbolic of municipal authority but not directly so; one may feel that one is paying for a parking service. The ambulance siren is immediately recognized by all as signifying an emergency. There is one purpose for its use—to get people out of the way. The gavel is associated with the judge while he is exercising vested authority. It is the most specific symbol of the group, for only a given type of person involved in a given type of action will use it.

6. What other symbols represent authority in this nation? (*Power:* tools; traditional authority; institutional authority)

Annotation

Some symbols representing authority are:

    a. The American flag representing the authority of federal government resulting from the union of the states.

    b. The eagle on the quarter and the dollar representing the United States Treasury. The eagle says, in effect, "Do not deface!"

    c. Uncle Sam representing the call for citizens to serve their country.

    d. A red cross on a white background representing medical aid on the battlefield. In war it means, "Do not shoot."

    e. Traffic lights representing the municipal authority or some road authority in the regulation of traffic, i.e., to tell pedestrians and drivers when to go and stop.

    f. The balancing scales representing judicial authority.

Are there other kinds of symbols which do not represent authority but which everyone understands the meaning of? (*Power:* tools)

Annotation

Some symbols which convey meaning other than authority are:

a. A candy-striped pole representing the barber shop.
b. The dove with an olive branch representing peace.
c. An *S* framed by a triangle representing Superman.
d. A white flag representing surrender.
e. The donkey and the elephant representing the Democratic and Republican parties.

7. Speculate with the children concerning why policemen may carry a gun, a nightstick, and handcuffs. (*Power:* institutional authority)

Annotation

The authority to carry guns, nightsticks, etc., is given to the policemen by the government.

To the extent that the government represents the people, the policemen's authority comes from the people. What is highly debatable is the extent to which the people are represented by the government.

8. Has the policeman the authority to use the gun, nightstick, and handcuffs when he is off duty? Could the policeman arrest a member of his own family? (*Power:* institutional authority. *Conflict:* intraindividual and individual-institutional. *Valuing:* priority valuing, overlapping contexts.)

The answers to these questions may vary widely depending on the extent of authority granted by government and permitted by the United States and/or state constitutions, as well as on the circumstances. The policeman cannot make an arbitrary arrest. He can arrest a member of his family only if the member has committed a crime. However, a conflict may arise within the policeman between his loyalty to his government and to his family.

Even society as a whole might not think it was right for the policeman to arrest a member of his family.

EXAMPLES OF MATERIALS
FOR THE SECONDARY SCHOOL

Element I for a Curriculum Packet on *Valuing*

Grade level: Tenth (with possible use in grades 9–12).
Source for topical input: The social science (political science).
Action-Concept: Valuing—Individual material; individual ethical; institutional ethical overlapping contexts, ahistorical contexts. While *Valuing* is the focus of this element, *Conflict, Power,* and *Interaction* are involved. These are especially present in the description of the situation as set forth in the leaflets.
Padagogical Media: Role production.

The following accounts of a situation,* which occurred in the mythical community of Bender, Indiana, are to be distributed to the students in leaflet form (prepared from master dittos supplied in the curriculum packet).

> *Leaflet I*
>
> *BACKGROUND LEADING UP TO*
> *THE GRAND JURY INDICTMENTS*

1963·
Former county commissioner John H. Black, Jr., was elected Mayor of Bender, Indiana.

1966
Mayor Black and the city council presented plans for what they termed a "golden age" for Bender which were to bring urban renewal and community interest back to the center of town.

---

*The facts recounted in this situation actually occurred in a city in Indiana.

1963–1970

A program to increase the water works facilities was
      completed.

A project to improve the sewerage system was undertaken.

New street lights were installed and sidewalks in the
      center were repaved.

A remedy for the city's parking problems was proposed.

The transformation of a major street into a car-free mall
      was proposed.

Property was acquired by the city in the heart of town for
      the construction of a high rise to include several
      stories of parking facilities, a residence for senior
      citizens, and numerous stores and businesses. The
      arrangement was to have a consortium of local
      churches to fund the construction of the high rise
      with financial aid made available by the federal
      government, providing that a deadline was met as
      set by the government.

1967

Mayor Black was reelected.

1970

A county grand jury, on complaint submitted by the
      Indiana State Board of Accounts, indicted Mayor
      John H. Black, Jr. and City Controller Howard A.
      Smith on five counts. These were:

Malconduct in office.

Failure to follow the State Board of Accounts' directives
      concerning accounting procedures.

Misapplication of city funds.

Misapplication of city government property.

Paying a warrant in excess of appropriation.

The indictments handed down referred specifically to two
      actions taken by the administration: the purchase
      of land for the high rise and the repaving of side-
      walks around the courthouse. The three parcels of

land, intended as site for the high rise, were purchased *before an appropriation was authorized.* According to Black this was necessary to meet the deadline set by the federal government for granting aid. The issuance of a warrant *in excess of appropriation* referred to the purchase of one of the parcels of land for $150,000. Misapplication of city government property was charged on the basis of the land purchase. The indictment stated that Black and Smith *misapplied $365,000* of city funds by issuing three warrants, "contrary to the ordinances of the City of Bender and the statutes of the State of Indiana." Malconduct in office was based on the claim that the sidewalk construction and the land purchases were *illegally paid for from the city's utility fund.* The charge of failure to follow the State Board of Accounts directives arose in connection with a *warning issued by the Board, which had gone unheeded,* that utility funds should be used only for utility projects. The charge of misapplication of city funds were based on a *statute which prohibits an official from allowing a claim (in this case, the payment for the land) against the city without the claim first being, "itemized and verified and filed in the office of the clerk and placed upon the claim docket at least five days before the session at which the claim is to be allowed."*

1971

Black and Smith brought to trial.

Black announces his candidacy for reelection.

Leaflet II

THE POLITICAL ARENA, 1963–1970

Mayor John Black's victory in the 1963 election was accompanied by an upheaval in Bender politics. Black's Republican ticket swept the incumbent Democrats from city hall. The mayor and the new city council considered themselves a team of "action" Republicans and did actually undertake to renew the urban center of Bender.

Due to an increase in population, the city council membership was expanded from seven to nine members and the mayor stepped down from the post of council chairman. This meant that the council chairmanship was elected by the council from among its own members. The team of "action" Republicans began to lose some of its cohesiveness. In subsequent elections, two of Black's close collaborators lost their seats on the council. Another of Black's collaborators lost his bid for reelection as council chairman and his successor, a Republican of the old guard, was considerably more critical of Black's program. The new chairman was particularly contrary to Black's proposal for a car-free mall and it was he who led the attack against the administration's handling of appropriations. It should be noted that the possible inconveniences to property owners along the proposed mall may have contributed to the defeat of some of Black's team. It was well known that Black and the state administration of the same political party were at odds over patronage and particularly over the two percent kickback which had been customary for city employees to pay into the campaign fund of the party in power. Black criticized partisan politics in government and opposed the kickback.

Leaflet III

ATTITUDES IN THE COMMUNITY
TOWARD THE INDICTMENTS

Citizens interrogated and quoted by the Bender *Herald* on September 20, 1970.

Citizen I: I'm a good Republican and I voted for Black but I wouldn't vote for him again.

Citizen II: Bender has grown so fast a lot of the public officials don't know how to handle it. I'm surprised there weren't others involved though. I'm very surprised at the controllers (sic)—he comes from a very good family.

Citizen III: I don't know all the facts yet, but I think it's pretty good that they (the grand jury) brought this information out into the open. I would like to see things cleared up as soon as possible so the confusion with the city government can be cleared up. It appears as if there may have been some shenanigans.

Citizen IV: It's regrettable that corruption has apparently reared its ugly head in Bender. I hope the matter will be brought to a speedy trial and Mayor Black and Controller Smith—if they are guilty—will be severely penalized.

Citizen V: I wasn't surprised, but the fact that an indictment was made will hurt both men around here—in my opinion—no matter how they're found in the court trial.

Citizen VI: I'm glad they got him (Black) on the parking high rise thing.

Citizen VII: It looks pretty bad. If the grand jury indicted them (Black and Smith) it sounds like it must be true. I always used to think Black wasn't too bad before the parking dispute, but now whatever he gets is okay.

City Attorney James Blair (cited in the Bender *Herald* on September 19, 1970): "I know of no other incident where a city official has been indicted on such charges as these where he himself or some other member of the administration had not personally benefitted."

On September 24, 1970, the Bender *Herald* published an article by Larry Benito with the following headline:

WHY DID SBA (State Board of Accounts) SINGLE OUT BLACK, SMITH?

Mr. Benito noted that the statute which authorized this grand jury also gave the state examiner, the governor, and the attorney general, "the privileged opportunity of secrecy, and of disclosing or not disclosing financial irregularities, in public accounts." Benito continues somewhat further on in his article, "It would indeed be interesting to know just how many public accounts of other cities in Indiana today show disparities, without criminal intent, similar to those in the public account which have brought these two highly respected Bender officials to the brink of personal, family, and political disaster."

On January 8, 1971, two city councilmen entered a statement on the council records lauding Black "for the great industry, selflessness and extreme dedication in promoting and meeting the needs of the city."

Leaflet IV

REACTIONS OF THE MAYOR TO THE INDICTMENTS (AS QUOTED BY THE BENDER HERALD)

Quote 1: Our record stands.

The projects were for the people and in the best interest of the community.

It was not for ourselves.

(September 19, 1970:

Quote 2: No one has taken any money, no one has embezzled any funds and no one has any conflicts of interest.

(September 19, 1970):

Quote 3: No government official, unless he has nothing to do or is in a community which is not growing, has been perfect.

(September 24, 1970):

Quote 4: The Bender *Herald* indirectly quoted the mayor as saying that the State Board of Accounts was required by law to do a yearly audit of city books, but that the SBA did not follow this law because sufficient funds for this purpose were not available. "It's all a matter of whose ox is being gored." (September 24, 1970.)

TEACHING SUGGESTIONS

(*Note:* Neither the sequence nor all the questions and activities need be followed for the content of this unit to be taught successfully. An open curriculum structure permits considerable adaptation of specific content.)

A discussion following the distribution and reading of the leaflets might evolve around the following questions and accompanying annotations.

1. Suppose the indictments handed down by the grand jury had concerned embezzlement. Would you consider this a more serious charge? Why? (*Valuing:* overlapping contexts; individual material. *Power:* institutional authority.) (*Annotation:* The most obvious response is that embezzlement is considered a crime of greater gravity and usually carries a more severe punishment than the misdemeanors listed against the mayor and controller. The real problem is that the mayor overextended his legal authority and thereby committed a crime against all the people of his community. Can such a crime, even if done for the good of the community and without personal gain, be considered less than embezzlement?)

2. If the mayor and the controller were not profiting from the financial transactions, should they have been brought to trial? (*Valuing:* overlapping contexts; individual material; individual ethical) (*Annotation:* There are other motives besides personal gain that can lead to violations of the law. It is an old unresolved question. Is a

public official ever justified in breaking the law even for the good of the people? We have been taught to serve the public and we have been taught to obey the law. We have also been taught that all men should be treated equally before the law—including public officials. There is an immense conflict of values apparent in the brief political saga of the mayor. The mayor's past record has shown that he has made a real effort to benefit the people of his community. The charges deal with mismanagement. The mayor, in one of his quotes (Leaflet IV), implies that such mismanagement is inevitable in a growing community. But did he really have the right to go around the law even for the good of the people? An elected official is one who is trusted to do what the law says. Did the mayor betray the electorate's trust?

While the students will probably try to grapple with the above problems, none of them can be resolved. A host of other questions arise. For instance, do the people owe loyalty to the law? What are the assets and detriments arising from strict obedience to the law? Can laws ever be taken at *face value* or must they always be reinterpreted? The United States Constitution must be continually interpreted. Why? Is this desirable? All of these questions should remain unsolved. None of us knows the answers—all of us have opinions.

The real point is to underline the conflicts which occur among the values that each one of us carries. These values have all been reinforced by our own cultural heritage and, yet, we frequently find that it is necessary to decide in favor of one set of values over another. That is, we are forced to assign priorities to our values. Mayor Black may have done precisely that. He may have looked at the financial and social well-being that an improved urban center would give to the people and then considered that well-being to be more valuable than strict adherence to laws concerning the administration of public funds.)

3. Do you think there might have been motives under-

lying the investigation of the grand jury other than a desire for strict adherence to the law? (*Valuing:* institutional ethical; overlapping contexts) (*Annotation:* In Leaflet III, the headline WHY DID SBA SINGLE OUT BLACK, SMITH? certainly hints that there were other motives. Mr. Benito noted in his article that bureaucratic mismanagement in Indiana is not unusual. The real question then is why were the administrators of Bender, all Republicans, picked out for legal action by a Republican state administration. The information supplied in the leaflets is not sufficient to reach a conclusive answer. The class would be engaging in speculation. After various possible motives had been gathered, the following question of priority valuing might be posed: "Do you think the motives of Black or those of his opponents were more honorable?" Even if the class is in complete agreement, it should be emphasized to them that they are speculating. A return to the third leaflet and the citizen's quotes could be used to underline how such speculation, without facts, could be unfair. Several of the citizens seemed to think that there was a question of corruption in the Black administration. One citizen felt that if there was an indictment, this meant that there must be truth in the charge.)

4. Are there absolute values, i.e., values that are true for all times and all circumstances? (*Valuing:* ahistorical contexts; overlapping contexts) (*Annotation:* This is a question that has been debated for centuries. Throughout time men have had certain innate needs. Food, shelter, and the need for security have been among these. Consequently, many human actions resemble each other. The golden rule, "Do Unto Others as You Would Have Them Do Unto You," has been found in vastly different cultures. It might be considered a universal value. But even so, the "doing unto others" takes such diverse forms in different social groups that the role seems to hold little of the truly absolute, of the truly perfect in it. If one would not be killed, he should not kill, but if one's whole life's

savings are being taken, would this not justify killing? In some societies it would, in some it would not. If one would be given food when hungry, should one not give food to those who are hungry? In a society where the majority are not hungry, this rule can be easily accepted, but in a society where hunger is usual and the individual with food would not be left with his own shirt by those who are hungry, the rule meets continual modification.

Certainly, a large segment of the United States' population accepts the concept of absolute values in theory. Most Christian ethics are based on a conception of that which is considered an absolute good. It is realized that the individual may not reach such perfection, but his effort in approximation is enough. Even in the Christian ethic, a sense of relativity has crept in. Joseph Fletcher's *Situation Ethics*[17] would have the Christian decide his actions relative to the circumstances. Again, no one has the conclusive answer. Each man must reach his decision on the basis of the best available knowledge.

It could be noted to the students that the same kind of value problem underlies the Black-Smith case. Would the behavior of these officials be reprehensible under any and all circumstances? Can the students think of circumstances under which the misdemeanors in question would be more or less grave?)

Role Production

Students are to be given, at random, descriptions of the roles they will plan in an open meeting to take place at the town hall before the mayor and controller are placed on trial. Some townspeople have requested the removal of the mayor and controller from office. The students must express their feelings supporting the position they have assumed. Among the roles to be played are:

[17]Joseph Fletcher, *Situation Ethics*, Philadelphia: Westminster Press, 1966.

The mayor
The controller
Several councilmen supporting the mayor
The council chairman against the mayor's program
The city attorney (see Leaflet III)
The newsreporter (see Leaflet III)
The seven citizens (see Leaflet III)
A member of the State Board of Accounts
The state governor
The three people who sold their land to the city
Several disgruntled persons living along the street to become a car-free mall
Several elderly persons who were to benefit from the high rise
A representative of the consortium of local churches

It might be profitable, after the distribution of the roles, to permit students to mill around the room, talking over their roles with their classmates and trading roles where both students agree to do so.

The teacher could also assign several research projects before the role playing gets under way. Among these might be:

The grand jury
The structure of the city government
The strict interpretationists versus the loose interpretationists in American history
Urban renewal: Is it the way of the future?

During the actual town hall meeting, the teacher will play the role of the impartial moderator, but spontaneous interruption by the role players should be permitted to make the setting more realistic and to add a strain of emotionalism that would be present in an actual situation. The role-playing session will be brought to an end

by the taking of a vote to remove or to retain the mayor
and the controller.

Element II for a Curriculum Packet on *Valuing*

Grade level: Tenth (with possible use in grades 9–12).
Source for topical input: Vague subverbal impressions
    and models of formal analysis.
Action-concept: Valuing—Individual-ethical; individual-
    material; individual-institutional; overlapping con-
    texts.
Pedagogical media: Advertisement.

The following advertisement, which appeared in the
student newspaper, *The Daily Illini,* on September 22,
1970, is to be distributed to the students as a handbill.

Want to Be Relevant?

JOIN

Young
Americans
For
Freedom

☆ ☆ ☆ ☆

Help Your
University
Help America;
Help the Free
Enterprise
System

TEACHING SUGGESTIONS

(*Note:* Neither the sequence nor all the phases suggested here must be followed for the unit to be a success. It is hoped that the teacher will adapt the suggestions presented here to the particular needs of his class.)

1. This advertisement is attempting to put the organization, Young Americans for Freedom, in a favorable light by building upon established, positive values. In our present times, concepts such as "relevance," "freedom," "free enterprise," and "helping America," connote positive values. Placed in a given context, they could assume negative values (e.g., the fruits of free enterprise are also the fruits of ecological destruction). However, if the context is not a clearly negative one, the use of these words adds a favorable aura to the entire thought.

To continue the development of this idea, the following lists of words, printed on large flash cards, may be randomly presented to the students. The words have been chosen for their favorable or unfavorable connotations. It should be noted that such connotations are debatable. The students would be requested to decide whether these words carry positive, negative, or neutral connotations when seen out of context.

Freedom	Youth
Obedient	Masculinity
Dedication	Allegiance
Average	Equality
Indifference	Garbage collector
Discrimination	Compromise

(*Annotation:* There will no doubt be considerable debate regarding the connotations to be assigned each word. Some, however, will excite more agreement than others. "Freedom," "dedication," and "equality" are most likely to be classified as carrying favorable connotations, while "indifference," "discrimination," and "garbage collector" are most likely to be classified as carrying unfavorable connotations. "Obedient," "average," "youth," "masculinity," and "compromise" should cause considerable debate, especially since the first four of these are in a phase of shifting from a favorable to an unfavorable context. For instance, "youth" used to be primarily associated with the pleasurable things of life. Its association with violence and riots is now developing because of the campus disturbances that this country has experienced. "Obedient"—a stance long rewarded in the schools—is becoming associated with lack of imagination or with being a "square." Other words which could cause considerable controversy are "Negro," "structured," "politician," and "activist.")

2. Once the students have made their selections, ask them to think of circumstances under which the connotations they ascribe to a certain word could be different or opposite. (*Annotation:* It should be emphasized to the students that all of the listed words are devoid of value unless they are related to a context and a criterion. Let us take "equality" as an example. If the relationship of men and women are under discussion and "equality" is advocated, it is meaningless unless the circumstances and the criterion are specified. The circumstances may refer to retribution for work and the criterion may be equal salary or equal work hours or, even, equal home care of children. However, if "equality" is to carry any real (as opposed to merely connotational) value in our society, the criterion and the context must be specified. What one is "dedicated" to, how one proposes to use "strength," and in what circumstances, etc., are questions which should be asked before a positive value of goodness or desirability is attributed to any concept. Such is often not the case. We attribute, unconsciously, positive or negative values to words that are out of context and have no related criteria. The advertisement distributed is an ex-

ample of words which have been disassociated from specifics and which have been used in an effort to convince on the basis of connotational values alone.)

3. Are there questions that need to be asked before a value is ascribed to a word or phrase? (*Annotation:* We need to ask *logically prior questions*, i.e., questions which must be asked and answered before a reasonable conclusion can be reached. If the statement is made, "I want law and order," before a positive value of "good" can be assigned to it, one must know in what context and according to what criteria law and order would be used. There is considerable law and order in a dictatorship as well as in a democracy. Furthermore, law and order may be more valuable in one situation than in another. Students could be asked to think of situations in which law and order would not be very valuable. Some examples are: (a) when minorities are oppressed; (b) when constitutional rights are curtailed by the enactment of a law; (c) when in-class creativity is discouraged; or (d) when necessary change is stifled.)

4. The following fill-in paragraph and accompanying instructions would be dittoed (from masters included in the packet) and distributed to the students. This activity is intended as a means of applying some of the ideas acquired in the preceding discussion.

Instructions to Students: Fill in the spaces with as many words as you think are necessary to make this paragraph either a favorable one to the audience described or an unfavorable one to them.

A meeting was held at the University of Illinois, and a

crowd of _____.

The speaker, a prominent _____, addressed

the audience about student concerns, and _____

————————————————————————————. Crowds of students

waited ——————————————— when he had finished.

It was a ——————————————— affair. The speaker

had to leave ——————————————— because he was ex-

pecting ——————————————————————————.

(*Annotation:* A comparison of the finished products would demonstrate to students how very different a paragraph with a similar structure and subject can be with merely the addition or modification of a few words.)

5. An in-depth analysis of the handbill advertisement is undertaken in this phase. The objective is to discuss the way bias has been covertly inserted in this apparently simple advertisement.

The following questions may be used to encourage initial discussion.

    a. Are you favorably impressed by this ad?
    b. Would you respond to it?
    c. What else would you like to know to respond favorably to it?

After the initial discussion, small cards upon which are printed the question, "Want To Be Relevant?" are to be distributed. An informal survey of the students' spontaneous reactions to the question could be used to arouse student involvement in this activity. The response to this type of question is usually, "Yes, But How?" A second set of printed cards are then to be distributed. Each card will present a different response to the question, "Want to Be Relevant?" Among the responses to be included are: "Study Foreign Languages"; "Fight Pollution"; "Give to the Needy"; "Work in the Peace Corps"; "Protect America from Its Enemies"; etc. Only one slip of paper would contain the phrase appearing in the advertisement, "Join Young Americans for Freedom." Each student should be requested to read his response to the question. Following this, the students should be asked to discuss the relative value of each response, judging, if they can, which of the responses carry more importance. Through this discussion, it is hoped that the students will come to realize that judging the relative value of the responses on the basis of the available information is done at the risk of gross inaccuracies. (*Annotation:* There is not enough information in the advertisement to decide if one or another response is more relevant or more valuable. While the students themselves may be the carriers of criteria, there is not sufficient context to judge any response. Some *logically prior questions* should be asked in order to acquire this context. For instance, the response "Help the Needy" should be further explicated by answers to such questions as, "Who Are the Needy in Question?" "What Are They Needy for?" "How Would Their Needs Be Satisfied?" "Is This Kind of Help Consistent with My Own Beliefs?"

The advertisement itself is misleading because it is not only responding to the question, "Want To Be Relevant?" but it implies that relevancy can be achieved in only one way when, in fact, there are numerous alternatives. Furthermore, the reader is led to believe that if he were a member of the Young Americans for Freedom group, he would be relevant. However, he is not furnished with any information concerning this organization. Before a conclusion or value judgment is reached, some *logically prior questions* should be answered.)

6. The students, at this point, would be encouraged to formulate *logically prior questions* of their own. Examples of such questions are:

   a. What are the objectives of Young Americans for Freedom?
   b. Why is membership in the Young Americans for Freedom group valuable?

    c. What are the methods to be used by this group in achieving their goals?

    d. Are the group's methods in keeping with my ideals?

    e. What is meant by "freedom"?

    f. What is meant by "relevancy"?

The in-depth analysis would be continued by requesting students to observe the lines, "Help America, Help the Free Enterprise System," in order to determine whether the reader is being led to hold as valuable that which he could not know is valuable from the available information. (*Annotation:* "Help America" tends to receive a favorable response from the reader. By placing "Help the Free Enterprise System" on the same level, with an equal stress, the reader is led to believe that helping free enterprise is equivalent to helping America. To go from one to the other is to imply a fallacious or irrelevant conclusion. Helping free enterprise does not necessarily lead to helping America. Indeed, there is empirical evidence that the contrary often occurs. For example, the operations of free enterprise have permitted the misuse of American ecological environment endangering the very survival of man. Actually, the specific content of this advertisement could be about anything. For instance, "Help Johnny." The same kinds of questions would have to be asked before action should be taken on the advertisement. The students should be requested to pose some *logically prior questions*, the responses to which are necessary before one can conclude that free enterprise will help America. Examples of such questions are:

    a. How does America need help?

    b. How does free enterprise need help?

    c. Is free enterprise a desirable concept for a modern nation in today's world? What are the characteristics that make it desirable? What are the characteristics that make it undesirable?

d. In what ways can free enterprise help America?

These questions would be as valid if "Johnny" were the object and not "free enterprise." The substitution would be:

a. How does America need help?
b. How does Johnny need help?
c. What are the things that make it desirable or undesirable to help Johnny?
d. In what ways can Johnny help America?

7. The advertisement stresses "relevance." Students could be asked the following questions:

a. What is "relevance"?
b. Why is "relevance" valuable?
c. Is it always valuable or are there instances when it is not valuable?
d. Why do you want to be relevant?

After a brief discussion concerning the value of "relevance," the following brief essay (dittoed from a master included in the curriculum packet) is to be distributed to the students as a stimulus for an in-depth discussion concerning "relevance."

Relevance

It may be said that what is "relevant" depends on what is vital for the individual or the societal way of life. A way of life, however, is not an absolute. Men do not all choose similar ways of life. They give importance to some things and not to others. Men value different ways of life.

To deal with the problems and urgent happenings of the times is relevant in an era that is concentrating all its efforts on the improvement of existing conditions. But if the present life is considered secondary to a life-after-death, the question of present problems becomes far less relevant. In the same way, a materially comfortable life may carry high value for some men and be of little consequence for others. Among certain American Indian tribes, material possessions are looked upon as detriments. That man is honored most who gives away his property. A high-paying job may, thus, be relevant or irrelevant according to what is, for the individual, valuable to his way of life.

"Relevancy" cannot be spoken of in absolute terms. To know what is relevant, one must first know what he considers most valuable. The attribution of importance and the recognition of priorities inevitably precedes the determination of what is relevant.

The following questions may be employed to further the discussion of the essay.

   a. What is usually meant when it is said that school is not relevant?
   b. Can you distinguish between intellectual relevance, social relevance, and personal relevance?
   c. Can it be said that it is more relevant to study for space exploration than for typing?
   d. What are the most relevant happenings of our times?
   e. What is the most relevant for you?
   f. Can there be conflicting relevancies?

(Annotation: The very last question may be used as the teacher's entry into a brief discussion of priority valuing. It is relevant to prepare oneself vocationally. Such relevance, however, does not carry with it a fixed or absolute value. A given specialization in engineering might make it possible to find an immediate high-paying job, while, in a not-too-distant future, that same job will be obsolete. Even if the individual compromises and prepares himself for both eventualities, he will still have to decide where to place his most vigorous efforts, i.e., on the job now at hand, or on learning the job that is to come. In the same vein, when a community decides to place all its financial support for a super highway to be ready some five years hence and does only minimal repairs needed on existing roads, it has made a choice among values. It has given its priority to future needs and, therefore, a higher value has been placed on the future than on the present. In effect, the community has said that it is more important to take care of future needs than present needs. The citizen may feel the opposite position would be the better one; that is, present needs should be taken care of before future needs. Another example (currently before the country) is the priority to be attributed to moon exploration, education, and poverty programs.)

8. The advertisement, as has already been demonstrated, uses the concept of "free enterprise" about as ambiguously as that of "relevance." The salient characteristics of "free enterprise" are unhampered competition with minimal government interference in the development of private business. The following expressions are typical of American rhetoric. They are to be printed on small-sized posters for presentation to the students who will judge whether the expressions are in keeping with more or less government control.

   a. Environmental pollution must be checked. (more)
   b. American industry produces the best steel in the world. (less)
   c. Costs are skyrocketing and must be brought under control. (more)
   d. You can't keep a good man down. (less)
   e. A man should be able to do what he wants with his own property. (less)
   f. It is imperative that small businesses be protected from the squeeze of giant industry. (more)
   g. Compulsory education must be maintained if the

high standards of this country are to be maintained. (more)

h. Expenditures for political campaigns should be limited. (more)

i. Given the chance to develop freely, talented men will show their abilities no matter what their socio-economic backgrounds are. (less)

j. Too often, rules and regulations hamper creativity not only in business but in all aspects of life. (less)

(*Annotation:* The students, after having considered the above expressions, are to be asked to find other expressions of a similar nature, supportive of or against government intervention in the affairs of private industry. Newspaper editorials are a good source of such expressions.

The above expressions may also serve as examples of how priorities shift, making what is less valuable in one context, more valuable in another context. For instance, steel-producing companies have contributed to the pollution of lakes because the large quantities of water available from the lakes simplify and economize the production of steel. Inexpensive steel has been highly valued not only by the companies but by the purchasers and other eventual users. Thus, the positive value given to clean water has been much less than the positive value given to the inexpensive production of steel. At present, these priorities are inverting so that unpolluted water is *more* desirable than inexpensive steel. Laws have been recently passed to control industrial pollution. To avoid direct government interference and to retain, at least apparently, the tradition of free enterprise, steel companies may voluntarily modify their production methods. Students could undertake research projects concerning the use of law to control pollution and its relationship to free enterprise.

It becomes clear from the preceding discussion that, in our society, free enterprise varies considerably in the positive value attributed to it. Free enterprise passes from one end of the scale of goodness to the other with amazing ease. It is not always considered good. It is not always considered bad. To present it in an advertisement as a desirable quality while ignoring the negative aspects is to create a highly biased writing.)

10 Evaluating the Broad Objective

Assuming that materials of the type envisioned in this work were introduced into the school, the problem of how to evaluate their effectiveness immediately comes to mind. The difficulty of such a task is increased by the complexity and range of the objectives involved. The objectives of social education are extremely complex for they span the acting of a citizen throughout his lifetime.

Evaluating specific behavioral objectives becomes more feasible as the characteristics of the objectives increase in their specificness and in their public observability. The more precisely the characteristics of desired goals can be described, and the greater the agreement achieved regarding each description, the more accurate the evaluation of the goal can be. Accuracy also increases as the period of learning involved shortens and as the number of factors influencing learning decline. Whenever more numerous and more complete observations are possible, it is logical to assume that the dependability of evaluations is increased. These comments do not diminish the importance of evaluating the achievement of broad, general, and even long-range goals. They are intended, rather, as recognition that evaluation must be understood within its limits both in the sense of what it is able to reflect and in the sense of how well it is able to measure that which it reflects.

It really means very little, as far as evaluation is concerned, to say that the aim of teaching is to modify behavior. Human behavior is always present no matter what the level of acting is, and its modification is an inevitable part of experience—*any* experience. Obviously, the fewer the experiences influencing the target behavior that occur during the learning period, the more accurate the evaluation of the teaching act can be. It is simpler to estimate whether Johnny has become a good typist than whether he has become a good citizen. The former presents a limited range of quantifiable, publically observable characteristics that are not prone to modifications due to daily experiences occurring outside the public school domain. The latter must be based on broad, encompassing characteristics that are highly general in nature, liable to considerable doubt concerning their meaning, and subject to far-reaching behavioral change due to experiences that are neither controllable nor foreseeable by the school. The mere discussion of the word "democratic" could involve all the scholars of our times without any agreement being reached. Even the concept of "active participation" may be confused by the political effect that abstaining from action can have.

If evaluation in social education is to succeed at all, the types of characteristics originating from the goals must serve as a guide to the formation of the evaluative criteria. In particular, the paucity of *specific* characteristics, both in the content input and in the outcomes, must be taken into account. The open curriculum structure requires an evaluative structure congruent with its nature as well as with its final goals. Specific sets of facts and/or principles are incidental to the broader goals. Knowing the contents of the United States Constitution does not, in and of itself, indicate that the citizen knows how to use the constitution in his daily living, or that he is capable of revising his models of governmental decision making so that the constitution becomes a malleable, changing instrument in his hands rather than a fixed, unchanging framework.

The evaluation of specific behavioral objectives assumes that such objectives in some way reflect the broader goals so that the positive evaluation of the one would imply the positive evaluation of the other. It is an assumption that must be continually investigated in the light of circumstances. For instance, it cannot be said that because an individual buys a daily newspaper he is politically knowledgeable. What he chooses to read is of crucial importance for it is doubtful that a daily reading of the comic strips would produce a more cogent political thinker. A proportioned categorization of his reading selections could yield some insight into the quality of his political thinking, but a true correspondence with the goal of political knowledgeability is still being missed. The quality of the individual's critical thought brought to his reading in a variety of political arenas must be at the crux of an evaluation that pretends to reflect the political knowledgeability of the citizen. Reading the daily paper may be accepted as indicative of intelligent political involvement of the citizen. Clearly, it could be a highly misleading criterion, for the quality of the citizen's political behavior cannot be estimated by the quantity of newspapers he handles. In other words, such an evaluation is not consonant with the nature of what is being evaluated.

The question of intellectual quality must be considered, and once this occurs a host of subjective doubts arise. In evaluating the increased quality of the citizen's decision-making capacity, the specific behavioral objective must deal with intellectual and attitudinal qualities that involve memorization and the like only secondarily. In such circumstances, the specific behavioral objective either becomes less describable and thus less specific, or it loses its capacity to reflect the broader goals of citizenship education.

The traditional subject, based on a discipline having a cohesive and systematic set of principles, has offered the public school a wealth of specific behavioral objectives. The system of grading, which has survived a series of fads and bandwagons, responds clearly to such questions as: How many facts does Johnny remember? How many principles does Johnny know well enough to apply? How well can Johnny express the principles in his own terms? As the preceding questions indicate, the specific behavioral objectives are based primarily upon a quantitative measure of the subject knowledge acquired by the student from the total quantity taught. So long as the subject taught does not pretend to cope with the frontiers of the discipline where the problems of scholars make everything uncertain, but rather depends on the knowledge that a discipline has already accepted as truth, congruency between evaluation based on grading and the goals of the subject studied can be achieved.

Congruency, of course, does not imply desirability. However, if it is desirable to evaluate the quantity of facts and principles that Johnny has retained, then present grading practices, frequently used as the basis for evaluating the success of educational goals, are not only congruent but desirable. A closed curriculum structure such as that based on the disciplines offers understandings and ways of behaving that are clear-cut and objectively describable. The feasibility of using the specific behavioral objective is thus greatly increased. A closed curriculum structure offers goals, which, at the public school level, are subject to summative or conclusive evaluations. A closed evaluative structure is simply one that can pose very precise, definable levels of achievement as the criteria for evaluation. Quantitative measures are easily adapted to the closed, evaluative structure. The less precisely the goals of study can be described, the more open, i.e., the more responsive to a variety of outcomes, the evaluative structure must be.

The discomfort which many educators have felt concerning the present grading system has arisen primarily from the realization that estimating the established quantity of facts and principles acquired by a student in no way estimates the student's ability to cope with the increasing complexities of the world he lives in. Coping is a qualitative not a quantitative question. There has been the growing realization that in order to evaluate the success of public schools in relation to the demands made on students in their daily lives, qualitative evaluation must be necessarily undertaken. The considerable dissatisfaction with the subject based on the discipline and the effort to make content more relevant (and more open) to life situations have emphasized the inadequacies of present grading practices, though little has been done to create an evaluative system consistent with the newer educational trends. Instead, quantitative evaluations have been applied in areas of study that are not disciplines. The term "subject" has been expanded to include areas of study such as language arts and social studies which are not based on specific disciplines. These so-called "subjects" do not present a specific set of principles from which the quantity of knowledge and the ability to operate with a quantity of knowledge can be profitably gauged. Structures may be superimposed on them for pedagogical purposes, but they, themselves, do not present a clearly defined unified organization generating specific kinds of knowledge. Certainly, English literature would go on generating even if the chronological ordering into Victorian, Romantic, etc., had not been devised. And the acting of citizens would proceed even without the open curriculum structure proposed in this work for the social studies.

The social studies was devised as a subject not because it was believed that given sets of principles existed which, when applied, would yield the best way of operating, but rather to prepare the student, as well as possible, to cope with his being a significant decision maker in a democratic society. It deals primarily with the quality of the citizen's involvement in public life—not the quantity. As noted previously, social studies is liable to a series of unpredictable experiences which influence outcomes and which require an open curriculum structure. Social studies is a subject by label only. It offers few specific behavioral objectives that would come anywhere close to representing its true goals. For instance, to estimate that a student reads voluntarily N number of politically inclined newspaper articles indicates no more than that a habit or an interest has been created. Certainly, such a habit or interest could exist equally as well in a totalitarian government, as even a superficial perusal of the *Pravda*, chock-full of political articles, would indicate. What is vital is the quality of the reading. How open, how critical, how creative is the citizen toward what he reads? How much commitment or active involvement is he prepared to contribute to his beliefs? As soon as such questions are asked—and they are the necessary questions in a democracy—the specificness of the goals diminishes into an open-ended vagueness of qualities that are desirable but difficult to define. Quantitative grades can communicate that a student needs more memorization or more exercise in acquiring a skill if he is to achieve a working knowledge of how a given established discipline operates. There is little effort to deal with student attitudes, personalities, and the like, which are at the very heart of evaluation in social studies. A closed evaluative structure based on quantitative measures ignores the qualitative input of both the students and of life itself.

The reworking of one's models and the processes of decision making are naturally dependent not only on the utilization of empirical data, but upon a host of factors including personalities, abilities, perceptions, interpretations, flexibility, openness, ethnic background, etc. Furthermore, these same characteristics must be considered in the teacher, for the more that qualitative aspects are evaluated, the more the subjective perspectives of the teacher are involved. In other words, the quality of the student's acting on given empiricals is funneled through the quality of the teacher's interpretation of that acting in his evaluation. The background of the teacher and the background of the student are intricately and necessarily involved in any evaluation of the social studies product. The evaluation of subjects based on disciplines has given us the illusion that all scholastic studies can be graded objectively by the teacher. A test based on 20 multiple-choice questions concerning the axioms or working principles of a discipline can certainly achieve greater objectivity than an evaluation of the citizen's critical involvement in politics. This is not to say that efforts to achieve objectivity in social studies evaluation should be abandoned, but rather that in order to achieve objectivity in evaluating outcomes, the subjective qualities must be recognized and the problem of translation into objective evaluation directly dealt with. It is avoiding the problem to pose a question of a quantitative nature which apparently achieves objective results (as in the case of letter grades), while ignoring entirely the subjective input of the evaluating teachers in those results.

Accepting the need for qualitative evaluation which takes the subjectivity of the evaluator into account, the problem now is one of how to achieve qualitative evaluation for a social studies program rooted in a democratic society and conceived within an open curriculum structure. The course suggested in this work has as its primary objectives the development of consistent, powerful, consciously held, and flexible models for significant decision making. Undergirding these qualities is the willingness to perceive new models and to change when models of improved quality appear. Qualitative evaluation of the proposed social studies course must be based on these objectives.

Two levels of evaluation are envisioned. The first would survey the responses of a large number of teacher-evaluators in a broad selection of situations and would employ consensus of opinions as the major data-gathering tool. The second would be considered a means of feedback to individual students and teachers during the learning period, and as a supplement to aid the teacher's judgment of student performance.

The survey or consensus evaluation is to be based on questions requiring "opinionated" responses. These questions would be submitted to a large sampling of teachers involved in a variety of socioeconomic situations. Crucial to the outcome of the evaluation is the quality of the questions to be utilized. To ascertain whether the willingness, as well as the ability, to conceive and accept change has been achieved, to determine whether consistency, awareness, logical power, flexibility, open-mindedness, and the generalization of models have been brought to greater maturity, the questions posed to teachers must reflect these objectives and not merely the extent to which specific content input has been assimilated by students.

Questions would require three levels of response, each dependent on a different base for comparison. The three bases would be:

1. According to the teacher's own norms; i.e., would the teacher be satisfied if this were the level achieved by his own flesh and blood?

2. According to the general achievement of the class; i.e., has the student achieved as well, not so well, or better than most of the students who have undergone the same learning experiences; has he progressed as quickly?

3. According to the student's own initial capacity and personality as perceived by the teacher; i.e., taking into account the unique qualities of Johnny, has he done well?

By establishing these three levels of response, subjectivity is certainly not escaped, but the teacher is led toward greater objective fairness when forced to compare his own norms with the norms of relative class achievement and with the norms dependent on the unique qualities and capacities of the individual student.

The following questions are conceived as being reflective of the objectives cited. The questions have been classified according to the objective that is being zeroed in on. As the objectives themselves are neither clearly defined nor mutually exclusive, the questions tend to overlap. Each of the questions requires the above-noted threefold response. In order to obtain a form of consensus, the responses are subdivided into multiple choices.

Open-Mindedness
1. Has the student developed his willingness to accept new and/or different ideas about himself, ways of acting, and the world around him?

Response I: According to Your Own Norms
a. Not at all up to my norms.
b. Not as much as I would consider satisfactory.
c. Satisfactory according to my norms but not especially outstanding.
d. Outstanding.
Response II: According to Overall Class Achievement
a. Compares poorly.
b. Compares not too far below satisfactorily.
c. Compares satisfactorily.
d. Compares very favorably.
Response III: According to Initial Student Capacity and Personality
a. No apparent maturation.
b. Less maturation than expected.
c. In keeping with initial expectations.
d. Far beyond initial expectations.
Note: The threefold, multiple-choice responses listed above would be used with each of the following questions but, for the sake of time and space, will not be repeated here.
2. Has the student increased his willingness to analyze his own actions and beliefs, as well as his identity, or place in the world?
3. Has the student increased his willingness to analyze the actions of others and the resulting influence upon the world around him?

Awareness and the Use of Logical Power
1. Has the student increased his capacity to discern problems and/or to predict future problems?
2. Has the student increased his capacity to find or conceive new and/or different solutions for problems?
3. Has the student matured in his ability to analyze his own actions and beliefs?
4. Has the student matured in his ability to analyze the action and beliefs of others?

5. Has the student improved his ability to search out required information?

6. Has the student improved his ability to evaluate the worth and relatedness of available information with regard to the problem at hand?

7. Has the student increased the types of logical analyses available to him (e.g., use of definition, formal consistency, logically prior questions, etc.)?

Flexibility

1. Has the student developed his willingness to suspend judgment and operate according to different methods of value orientations?

2. Has the student increased his ability "to change tracks," that is, to switch from one approach to another?

3. Has the student increased his ability to recognize when a new approach is needed?

The Achievement of More Generalized and Powerful Models

1. Has the student matured in his understanding of the possible uses of theory in everyday life?

2. Have the student's models or beliefs regarding his own life style undergone modifications as far as you, the teacher, are able to discern?

3. Has the student moved toward more maturity in his generalizations?

4. Has the student developed his ability to distinguish between value models and factual models?

5. Has the student developed his ability to grasp life models foreign to his own?

6. Has the student increased his ability to support his beliefs with facts, logical input, and value orientations when confronted with models not of his persuasion?

Data from the above questions would be obtained from the three-level responses. The possible statistical manipulations of the data are many. Numbers, of a ranking nature, could be assigned to each response and the sum of the responses from all categories and response levels could be averaged for all students involved. The results would then be based on the averages achieved by the students, as derived from the consensus of teacher opinions. A consensus of averages could be obtained according to objectives as well as according to response levels. Differences between response levels and total responses could be analyzed. A comparison of responses based on objectives and those according to response levels could be undertaken. The flexibility in possible statistical analyses is very promising of considerable objectivity, notwithstanding the highly subjective input of individual teachers.

This survey of teacher opinion with regard to the qualitative progress of students would be supplemented by in-class evaluative procedures which would offer the teacher more objective feedback than his own perspectives might permit. It must be clear by now that the quantitative grading, used widely for in-class evaluative purposes, is not only unreflective of qualitative goals, but forces the teacher to take the false position of a judge who can objectively estimate the worth of the student's qualitative output so closely bound up in ethnic background, socioeconomic status, language capabilities, personality traits, opinions, and so forth. In communicating such judgments, what can be achieved but the suppression of student qualities so that the student will conform to the qualities seen as "good" by the teacher? Suppression of individual qualities by one institution of a democratic society, which is what occurs with grading, is contradictory to the very essence of the social studies course proposed here. It is rather hoped that individual qualities will themselves grow through the support and encouragement of the course's established objectives. This is the essence of the open curriculum structure. The elimination of grading is not only proposed but recommended.

In-class evaluation that omits the quantitative stamp of approval or disapproval is, however, an excellent means for helping the teacher to objectify his views of student development. Yet, with or without grades, considerable care must be taken if *honest* student response is to be achieved. Students tend to act in conformity with what they believe the teacher wants. Quantitative grading reinforces this tendency. To avoid present excesses, it is necessary that evaluative exercises not only contribute to the objectification of the teacher's personal views, but guide the student to be open-minded, aware, more logically inclined, and flexible. Test forms must be conceived which, while using specific factual input, make such input secondary to the major objectives. Even traditional testing formats may be manipulated so as to achieve such ends.

The multiple-choice test is a highly favored, widely used means of obtaining grades and evaluative data concerning the success of materials. The multiple-choice format could be adapted to yield data concerning qualitative social studies objectives. Instead of having four choices, one of which best responds to the question, students would be presented with a series of choices, any number of which would be suitable responses to the question. Moreover, students would be given the opportunity of proposing additional, suitable replies to the question. Indeed, student supplementary responses would be encouraged. The greater the number of reasonable responses seen by the student, the more it could be assumed that the major goals of the materials (i.e., open-mindedness, flexibility, awareness, logical power, and control of more generalized models) had been achieved. The student who could find no correct answer among the proposed responses, could still be encouraged to offer his own version, and to the extent that his own versions were reasonable, flexible, open-ended, etc., they would contribute to the teacher's evaluation of the student's progress. On the other hand, the student who could think of no additional responses would still have a certain critical involvement in making his choices, for there would be neither a specific number of choices nor a specific number of acceptable responses presented, and he would know this.

The following are samples of the kinds of multiple-choice questions which could be adapted to in-class evaluative use by the social studies teacher. The materials supplying the specific content input concern the accusations brought against Mayor Black and City Controller Smith (see Chapter 9).

MULTIPLE-CHOICE QUESTION NO. 1

Other cities in the state show accounting discrepancies, but their officials have not been indicted. How does this fact bear on the indictments against the mayor and the city controller?

a. Since the officials of these other cities were not indicted, there may be political or even personal reasons underlying the indictments brought against Mayor Black and his city comptroller.

b. The State Board of Accounts has no business investigating the accounts of all the cities of the state.

c. The statute, which authorized the grand jury investigation, gives the state examiner, the governor, and the attorney general, the legal authority to ignore financial irregularities.

d. There is no cause to proceed against financial irregularities unless there is criminal intent.

e. It would be impossible to enforce the statute in every city of the state.

f. Other possible answers: ————————————

————————————————————————————

————————————————————————————

Annotation for Teacher's Use

Responses a, c, and e are acceptable. The student who selects all three has a broader, more flexible grasp of the materials studied than those who select only two. If none, or only one of the acceptable responses is chosen, then the student has not acquired the conception of a law whose application depends upon the judgment of one or two authorities. In particular, the additional power that is given to the authorities to act personally against political enemies has not been grasped.

There are a number of reasonable replies that could be added to those presented. For instance:

a. The other cities of the state have succeeded in hiding their financial discrepancies.
b. The financial discrepancies found in Bender were worse than in other cities.
c. The governor, or the state examiner, or the attorney general, or all three have cause to fear what the mayor and the city controller of Bender want to do, and the political power they might acquire.

As can be noted by the additional student responses suggested, such responses may be hypotheses, and need not be very profound (though this, of course, is desirable). What is vital is the student's ability to look at the question from views not handed to him on a platter. This is central to the judging of open-endedness, awareness, and the ability to achieve mature generalization. If the student is unable to choose the correct responses but does succeed in offering his own suggestions, he may not have grasped or studied the details of the specific content input, yet still have achieved attitudes and abilities consonant with the major goals.

> *MULTIPLE-CHOICE QUESTION NO. 2*
> The mayor's victory in 1963 swept his ticket into office. For a while, the city council operated as a team, but then the team began to fall apart. What happened?
> a. The members of the city council began to fight each other for political gain.
> b. The increase in the number of council members and the defeat of two of the mayor's close collaborators diminished the cohesiveness of the city council.
> c. The city council members who supported the mayor disagreed about major aspects of the mayor's program.
> d. The council chairman was not a supporter of the mayor, even though he belonged to the same political party.
> e. The mayor's supporters were disillusioned when he was indicted by the grand jury.
> f. The financial questions split the team.
> g. Other possible answers: _____
> _____
> _____

Annotation for Teacher's Use

Responses b and d are acceptable, and f is uncertain. Since it is not clear "what financial questions" are being referred to in response f, there is a hypothetical possibility that the response is correct. The teacher could assume that f was incorrect, and, if argument ensued (hopefully), yield to the student's contentions. The students who have chosen b and d (perhaps f) have grasped the overall political situation. They are aware of the factors involved in the diminished cohesiveness of the mayor's team, as presented in the materials.

There are a number of reasonable replies that could be added to those presented.

   a. When the mayor was chairman of the council, he had more control over the actions taken by the council.

   b. Public opposition to the mayor's program may have contributed to the election defeats of some of the team members, and the remaining members were not as willing to go along with the mayor for fear they also would lose their bids for reelection.

   c. The democrats were succeeding in their efforts to undermine confidence in the mayor.

MULTIPLE-CHOICE QUESTION NO. 3

The mayor and the city controller were not acting with criminal intent. Why were they indicted by a grand jury?

   a. Although they had no intention of doing so, the two officials embezzled large sums of money to start their new program.

   b. An action may be illegal without having criminal intent.

   c. The statute regulating financial management among the cities of the state makes financial mismanagement a criminal offense at all times.

   d. It is not up to the grand jury to decide criminal intent.

   e. Financial mismanagement of city funds is enough grounds to bring an indictment.

   f. Other possible answers: _____

_____

_____

Annotation for Teacher's Use

Responses b, d, and e are acceptable. In choosing the three, the student's understanding of the distinction between illegal action and action with criminal intent is ascertained, revealing, in particular, the ability to apply logical consistency within a political context.

There are a number of reasonable replies that could be supplied by the students.

    a. One may be moral and illegal at the same time.

    b. All the grand jury says with an indictment is that a judge and people's jury are needed to make a decision about intent, guilt, and the degree of guilt.

    c. There was so much public opposition to the mayor and the city controller before the grand jury was composed to decide the question, that the jurors were unfavorably influenced.

MULTIPLE-CHOICE QUESTION NO. 4

What are the values that can be seen operating and conflicting with each other in the case of the mayor and the city controller?

    a. One who works for the good of the community and without selfish motives is to be admired.

    b. The law must be equal for everyone no matter what position in the community is held.

    c. The law must be equal for everyone no matter what their intent is.

    d. The law should not be permitted to place stumbling blocks of a bureaucratic nature in the way of worthwhile public programs.

    e. If democracy is to work, no one individual or group should decide what programs are sufficiently worthwhile to ignore the established laws.

    f. If a government no longer responds to the needs of the people, the people have the right to overthrow the government.

    g. Other possible answers: _____

_____

_____

Annotation for Teacher's Use

Responses a, c, and e are clearly acceptable in the light of the facts presented concerning the indictments of the mayor and the city controller. Response b leaves something to be desired, since the statutes involved concern only particular positions in community government and therefore only certain individuals. However, any individual holding that office should be treated exactly like any other individual holding that office. In this sense response b is an acceptable response.

Responses d and f may seem acceptable to students who believe in the principles set forth in the Declaration of Independence, and who have not yet gained command of logical tools in analyzing governmental actions. In response d, the use of the word "worthwhile" is misleading. Who is to determine what is "worthwhile"—the people or the mayor? So-called "stumbling blocks," another propaganda-type phrase, may be the legal means to protect the people's right to determine what public programs are worthwhile.

Response f makes an unsupportable leap in logic. From one instance, in which a group led by the mayor has unsuccessfully attempted to put through a program, it cannot be concluded that the government no longer responds to the people. There is no evidence that the unsuccessful group represents all or a majority of the people even *in this one instance*. Certainly, more evidence than this case must be presented to sustain that the government does not suit the needs of a majority of the governed.

There remain a number of reasonable replies that could be presented by the students.

   a. An elected office holder should not forget that he is a member of a political party. He should work to keep his party united. He should not divide his party by pushing for programs unpopular with members of his own party.

b. It is not right for the law to permit elected officials to *personally* decide when another official should be prosecuted under the law and when he should not.

c. The people have a right to expect that their tax money will be spent legally.

The four multiple-choice questions presented above make it possible to deal, in an objective fashion, with subjective input. Exercises comprised of similar questions and approaches, which would receive no letter grade, could be useful not only as feedback for the teacher but as the basis for in-class review discussion. Talking answers over, letting students propose their own answers, letting students win some of the arguments that might arise over acceptable answers, reflect the underlying goals of the social studies program proposed in this work. The qualitative development of the student is also being directly dealt with. The success or nonsuccess of the enterprise will need time for the telling.

72 73 74   7 6 5 4 3 2 1